1

The Dirty Political Game

"My Life"

Authored by: Abdoul S Ouatthema

Created by: Ouatthema Intel

Published by: Ouatthema Intel

Printed by: createspace

Distributed by: amazon on amazon.com

Preface

Dedicated to my father, my first Drill Seargeant El-hadj Ouattara hema Bakary, retired custom border officer who still live in the West African Country of Burkina Faso. To my mother Aminata Ouattara hema my first lady, may her soul rest in peace "I love you mom". I wish long life to my Dad until I come back home from this so long journey abroad in the United States of America. I pray God to bless me with the strength to apologize to him for my stubbornness but also, pray God to give him as well the wisdom to recognize my courage and determination in life to reach my goals. My message to him would be "Dad it was hard, but I've made it". To my step sister Kadiatou Ouattara hema I've lost in 2011 while in America "May her soul rest in peace". Thanks to everyone who contributed or will contribute to make this book a success and help share this challenging but very rich life story with the world.

Summary

Results matters to me
and
I always have them

-Abdoul S Ouatthema . . . . . .

Understanding Life

Life is a gift from our creator perceived differently depending on our personal or religious believes. To live is just like to drive a car in a street traffic and we're all drivers of our own lives. Good drivers are the most successful and bad drivers always crash leading them to failure in life. While you drive, you encounter traffic lights and stops (corresponding to obstacles, laws, rules, regulations). When you get to a stop, you must decrease your speed look at the mirror then proceed with caution. Once you stop, it becomes very hard for you to get back to your normal speed. But once you find your normal speed from which you decelerated before the stop, it becomes easier and much comfortable to drive. In that traffic, you should expect other drivers on your way from each line of the street.

Your car could also get hit by another driver no matter how well you drive because in that traffic, not all drivers have a driver's license. Some might be intoxicated, unlicensed or inattentive. Rules are fixed by God and written inside the holly books like the bible and Coran. Those who crash have their license revoked and that is when you die. A driver's license is a privilege not a right because it can be canceled or revoked at any time so is life.

Also, your ability to efficiently drive, properly accelerate and decelerate depends on the state of the engine. In real life, we talk about health. The healthier you are, the better your life will be. It is important to regularly feed your body for better performance in life just like it is to put gas in your car. Doctors are engineers of our lives so whenever we encounter problems we contact them to diagnose and repair whatever went wrong.

The only difference between driving a car in a traffic and living your life is that your car's engine can be replace entirely with a new one while your body once damaged cannot be entirely replaced. That is when your life ends .....

That's my modest understanding of the life that we live here on earth and I wish good luck and safe trip to everyone driving their cars.

The Power of Your Words

I came to realize that the mind was a very powerful weapon so is your words. If not wisely used, they can create unimaginable destruction to you and to your surroundings. Those who realize such power in their life, try to think positively and talk less so that they can direct that powerful energy toward improving their conditions. If not wisely used they always come back to the sender in a form of self-destruction. Be careful using your words as they can do more harm than you can ever imagine.....

A Poem to My Woman

My heart, my life, my everything

My light, my protection, my inspiration

My only one, my woman, my señorita

What a beauty that shines my days

What a smile that lights my mood

What a smell that perfumes my clothes

For you I joined the army strong

For you I obtained secret clearance

For you I time traveled to Colorado

For you I unconditionally love

Now look at me, I am a success story

Now look at me, I am a leading power

Now look at me, I am the happiest man

You're my woman, my blond hair señorita

-To My Woman-

The Soldier's Poem

It feels like I am immortal

It feels like I'll never die

It feels like I solely exist

It feels like the sixth dimension

Time seems so senseless, life so customized

Things seem so perfect and premeditated

Everything seems to be right here, right now

21

It is so mysterious, so strange and so magical

What if it really is how it seems to be

What if nine eleven never happened

What if the President was the most dishonest

What if it was all lies, life just a dream

What if it was the American dream

I'll no longer be a soldier my military service will be

missed for ever

-Soldier For Life-

A thought to the homeless

The homeless, the invisible

The haunted by police force

The harassed by law enforcement

The sinner of religion

He's just poor he's not a homeless

He asks for help, he's not a criminal

What if you were wrong

What if the world was a home for him

If lie to be a crime

If sex to be a blame

The world would be a prison

The President a gangster

God would be the judge, Jesus an attorney

They'd be billions of convicts

I'll no longer be a soldier

My military service will be missed for ever...

The Soldier's Common Sense

"my common sense won't allow me to"

I am a soldier

Train to destroy

Hired to kill the enemy

Deployed to protect the innocent

I can't be a soldier, I once stole a water bottle

I am a criminal, I once stole a piece of bread

I no longer exist, I've been a homeless

I lost my sense of common being that soldier

Drill sergeant stole my freedom being that soldier

The Government prosecute because I am intelligent

I rather be a prisoner, not that soldier

I rather be a rebel, not that soldier

I'll no longer be a soldier

My Military service will be missed for ever. . . .

-My Common Sense-

A Trip To Freedomland

When time comes

When whistle blows

They'll be no time but life

You'll witness loneliness, sadness in the air

You'll see alike faces in your surrounding

The devil will celebrate, the angel indifferent

Death will be rushing, god will be watching

You're the only one in your world

When that time comes, don't you worry

You're just traveling to freedomland

Where everything is seen, everything is known

You just became a citizen, the one of freedomland

The devil is now desperate, the angel will now celebrate

Then God will proclaim, and you'll be free for ever . . . . .

-My Land-

Toilet Paper's Story

One of my best story is the one of toilet papers. They are

among the most disrespected and neglected things in life.

But nothing protects us better against our own odor than a

toilet paper. Once we finish using it, they're always flushed

inside a toilet or thrown inside a trash can. The funniest

thing is that we always need one if we don't want to stink.

Personal Quotes

. Good work is never wasted

. There is no bad result in life for whoever learn good lessons from it.

. Focus on the possible is the best way to turn the impossible into possible.

. Know the difference between right and wrong and live by these rules is the best religion on earth.

. Nightmare is nowhere far from wherever dream comes true.

. The secret to success is to do what you love, then love what you do.

-My quotes-

Life in Burkina Faso

Abdoul Saa'madolmi Ouatthema, born on April 25, 1981 in the west African Country of Burkina Faso. Burkina Faso is a landlocked country situated in West Africa with around 274,200 square kilometers (105,900 Square miles) in size. It is surrounded by six countries: Mali, Niger, Benin, Togo, Ghana and Ivory Coast. The city of Ouagadougou situated right in the middle on the map is the political capital of Burkina Faso. Its population was estimated at over 17.3 million in 2014. The country's official language is French because the country has been a French colony before it took its independence on August 5 1960.

Formerly called the republic of Upper Volta, the country was renamed Burkina Faso on 4 August 1984 by then-President Thomas Sankara. With more than 60 ethnic groups, 70 languages are spoken in the Country. Among the spoken languages we have Moore, Dioula, Bissa, Gourounssi, Gouin, Peuhl, Karaboro, Dagari, fulfunde, etc.....

As of today, the Country, Burkina Faso/Upper Volta has known the total of heights Presidents and three transitional Presidents. The current head of state is President Rock Mark Christian Kabore.

I spent my early life in the second city of the Country called "Bobo Dioulasso" where my family and grand-parents lived and worked for many years. From the Gouin ethnical group of Burkina Faso, my ancestors are from the West region of the country with the city of Banfora as capital. I am from a family of nine in total. Three sisters, two brothers and three step sisters. My dad was a custom border officer who served in the French Army back in days and my mom a social worker when I started kindergarden at "Denbagnouman" located in the borough of "KOKO". Before that, I was enrolled in an Islamique religious school for kids to learn how to read and write in Arabic. Then I started the modern French educational system in my first grade at the age of six in 1987 at "South Accart-ville preschool".

I grew up just like any other kids who don't get to choose but follow whatever is decided by their parents as ways for success. Along with other young kids we were sometimes forced to go to school and most of the time beaten or escorted to the classroom's door. Going to school was a big deal for us at some point because we feared the teacher who never hesitate to use his wood stick when we fail on a task or a test. A real nightmare it was at that early age in life. The same thing happened to all kids born and raised within that educational system zone in Africa except those from wealthy families that had a chance to attend fancy schools created and financed by western countries like France, Belgium, Switzerland etc..... Like any other west African Kid, I grew up playing soccer which was the main sport of the Country and didn't play basketball until my seventh grade (corresponding to college in the French system). I was part of young pioneers group of Burkina Faso under President Thomas Sankara, a program created by the Government to teach Military values to young people at the early age. While in service, we walked miles to surrounding villages and recite military creeds along the way.

Young pioneers of Burkina Faso under

President Thomas Sankara

While in Bobo Dioulasso, I hang with a lot of friends in the community and most of the times come late at home after school and didn't get to shower until late at night. Such behavior was also sanctioned by a consequent punishment at home by Dad or mom. We more often take the risk to break the rule by enjoying that so precious free time after school on our way back home. That free time was also an occasion for us to handle our dissensions and disagreements during class by some one on one or sometimes a group fight.

There's always a fight going on somewhere after class in the street on our way back home. In class, the older student, more likely the strongest was nominated as the chief by the teacher because he would be the most feared therefore respected. The chief is responsible to keep students quiet when the teacher is absent, make sure everyone does their tasks as assigned. He makes sure that the classroom get swept and sometimes moped, the board wiped up every morning before class. He is required to report anyone who refuse to execute to be sanctioned. As a reward from his position, he gets fame, authority, some privileges and exemption from some types of tasks.

My dad has served in the French Army when the Country was still a French colony and was a very good custom border officer I've heard from many sources loyal, honest, and hard working. Just like anyone who do such job of law enforcement he happened to have issues with the city's businessmen for refusing corruption, illegal drug trafficking, money laundering and many different crimes in Burkina Faso.

After retirement, my dad created his own export-import company in Ouagadougou with couple of young men that he hired. It all started when I was a fourth grader from our house garage before they moved their office in the center city. The company ended up being maliciously filched by a businessman citizen of Togo, friend of the dictator President Blaise Compaore and his brother Francois Compaore. The case was still pending in court when I left my Country.

44

The corrupt judicial system of Burkina Faso would always postpone the sentence and force him to spend all his money in documents and filling fees.

My dad has helped a lot of people however later in life and treated others sometimes even better than his own kids. Many family members and even people unknown to us where brought in our house, became successful then left. I happened to blame him for not privileging his own children seeing the opposite in other families. But I came to understand that it was his own and personal way to educate his children. Then my goal became not to get him change his way but to find my own way. However, it all proved me that, despite the complex nature of his lifelong profession he was human and a laying back person. As a director of the custom border department in Burkina Faso, my dad was relocated to the political capital "Ouagadougou" then he has moved with half of the family mostly my older brothers, sisters and step sisters.

The family was divided at some point because my dad has divorced my mom to live with my step mom in Ouagadougou. I stayed with my mom and both of my younger sisters until my time came for me to move as well and join them. The reason why I finally moved to Ouagadougou was because I was reported to my dad by his visiting friends to be stubborn, not studying and not listening to my mom anymore. Which I believed inaccurate because I was just living the normal lifestyle of any other toddler of my age at that time.

However, it wasn't a bad idea for me either because I also wanted to discover the first city of the Country, the capital and enjoy the new and more interesting life that my older brother and sisters lived. In 1990 all I remember, is that I traveled to Ouagadougou on a school break that goes from July to October and never came back to Bobo Dioulasso. The same year, my dad retired then we had to move from the Government premise to his own house that he had built on the peripheries of the city far from the center city, the part of the city which wasn't exploited

47

by the Government yet. There was no light or water installed in that area yet. An entire change in life style, not obviously what I was showed or expected when I left my mom with both my sisters to stay with them. We used lamps as electricity to study at night and get water from water fountain dig dip on the ground.

I was very controlled, watched, isolated and never enjoyed as much freedom as other kids in my environment. Even though I did not like that lifestyle, I still thought it was because my parents wanted me to be different and be successful in life so it was all good to me. I graduated in 1992 with an excellent grade and scholarship then entered college. The same year, my mom was diagnosed with a cancer which resulted in her right leg being amputated. Even though she was divorced she was then forced to move to Ouagadougou with my two little sisters while following up on her health. It was painful for me to see my mom, a beautiful smart and laying back person who spent her life helping others go through this situation. Her health went from bad to worst and she died at the hospital in March 1994 "May her soul rest in peace". I remember to have visited her couple of times at the hospital after my "taekwondo" training sessions. I traveled about 5 miles late at night just to see her at the hospital and make sure that she was going to come back home.

Late at night, around two in the morning on the 25th of March 1994 I suddenly woke up to find my dad sitting on the edge of my bed inside the room that I was sharing with both my older brothers. He was there to announce the shocking news that our mom has passed away at the hospital. That night just stayed indelible in my mind because it announces a new and very critical turn that was about to take place in my life and thus forever. I was even more shocked watching her being buried inside that hole and covered with sand and dust in that cemetery located couples of miles away from home on the west side of the city. What else could've I done I was thinking???..........Unfortunately nothing but to remain strong and deal with my new situation for the

50

rest of my life. Years later, I sometimes visited her grave alone to pray and talk with her….. I was convinced that she was able to hear and see me through my pain and realize how bad I missed her and needed her back. It hasn't been easy at all because right after, I started seeing a strong and negative impact in my life maybe because I was too young and so close to my mom. First in school, my grade started to significantly decrease but also socially my relationship with my step mom and dad degraded. I started repeating all my classes and hardly moved from one class to the next. It was hard but never impossible because I finally graduated from high school in 2004 then entered the University of Ouagadougou school of Economics and Management despite my personal social situation but also despite the negative Impact of the political environment "Dictatorship under Blaise Compaore" on education at the time.

I've been a very brilliant student until my mom's death then I became average always managed to pass my classes no matter how long it takes. Socially, I was very misunderstood especially by my dad who also changed and became more radicalized than ever maybe because of his deepened adherence in Islam. At some point, and most of my life It was his way or no way... I call him my first drill Sergeant... A drill sergeant who also had to deal with a stubborn soldier making the training very hard to handle in the first place.

After two years spent in college (University of Ouagadougou), between student strikes and political turmoil under a very contested dictatorial regime, I decided to emigrate. I knew that my future will be somewhere else than in this Country. Like always, I started my project by investigating a little bit on possibilities.

I visited the United States embassy in Burkina Faso couples of times then decided to apply for a student visas. A student visas because not just that I wanted to emigrate but I also wanted study and get a college degree like most students of my generation. The only problem was finance because I also knew that it takes a lot of money to study in the United States. But I thought I would be able to get a job, work and pay my tuition.

In order to obtain a simple admission letter at one of the United States University the student has to provide many documents like high school diplomas, transcripts and bank statement as proof of financial sufficiency. At first, I approached my dad who didn't even want to hear about my project then I realized that I had to find my own way which I did. Couple months later, I obtained my passport and sold my motorcycle for cash because I was convinced that it'll work the way I'd planned. At the big surprise of everyone (friends and family members), on the 24ht of August, I obtained my visas to follow my dream in the United States of America. To obtain an American Visas on my own was one of the biggest accomplishment of my life in Burkina Faso.

I admit to had been helped however at the very end of my struggle. My brothers and sisters started cooperating just 48 hours before my departure for the United States. I still remember this day like it was yesterday and I am grateful to my brothers and sisters no matter what happened between us they were there to help and support. I still believe the situation could've been better if they cooperated and helped a little bit earlier. My older brother offered me his suitcase to pack my clothes in, another gave me the equivalent of ($90 Us Dolllar)/(45,000 CFA) and my sister withdrawn $2000 for my plane ticket. I remember to have been trying a reservation with Air France at around 9:00PM for an 11:00 PM departure. It was so precipitated and emotional......

The only thing I regret is the lack of time that I had to announce and celebrate with friends and family one of the biggest event of my life. I wanted to celebrate the most important event of my life before I leave my Country with prayers and blessings from friends and family. I just didn't want to leave my country like a fugitive because I never intended to run away from no laws in my life and had never been convicted of any crime. It was only me and two of my sisters at Ouagadougou International Airport minutes before registration. I have used my last prepaid phone credit at the Airport to call close friends who weren't yet aware of the new situation then I gave my little prepaid phone to my sister. That was pretty much my last gesture toward my family and next thing, I was inside the gate waving them to go face my destiny. Where was I really going and would I be back home? ......I had no real idea beside what I see on television and I still don't know as of today but I was sure to be going to face my destiny on my own. I am here in the United States convinced that it'll happen. I am convinced that one day, sometimes very soon I'll be back in my Country like a hero.... this time, to reconcile with friends and family and celebrate my new departure to the United States as I wanted to.

My decision is taken however, I've decided to live in the United States as a naturalized citizen as long as the USCIS (United States Citizenship and Immigration Services) allows me to. meanwhile I still love my native country Burkina Faso and will always travel back and forth to visit friends and family. But most importantly, I want the American officials to understand that I am not a fugitive from my Country nor would I be one in the United States of America.

Foreign Student in America

I entered the United States of America for the first time in my life to face my destiny in the unknown as an international student with an F-1 status. I landed at the John F Kennedy Airport in New York City on August 25th 2007 at around 4:00 PM after almost 24hours long flight via Paris. As an international student, I was required to report to school as soon as I arrive in the United States. Even though I did not have enough fund to pay for tuition at the time, I remained confident that I would be able to get a job, work hard to pay my tuition. I always believed in opportunities and thought that If others did it then I can do it too. The greatest country on earth is the image that the country shows around the world through Hollywood anyways.

Once in America, I thought it would've been a good idea to first go to my friend's family in Philadelphia who emigrated just couple of years before me so that I could have an idea on the new life and system I was getting into. I stayed in their house couple weeks then had to go to school in order to keep my student status and remain legal in the United States but before, I also went back to New York to visit my cousin who also emigrated a year ago. I received many advices from both sides as well as from many African immigrants. But above all my own decision should prevail. Aware of and confronted personally with the new American reality, I had to take my own decision which I believed would be the best because no one know me more than I do myself.

On the first middle of September 2007, It took me over 24hours to travel from New York to Beckley in the State of West Virginia by the well-known American ground transportation bus company "Greyhound". Beckley is a beautiful small city in the country seat of Raleigh County in the States of West Virginia, United States. It was founded on April 4,

1838. The city was named in honor of John James Beckley, who was the first clerk of the house of representatives and the first librarian of congress. Beckley was founded by his son Alfred Beckley (United States Army general and confederate militia commander born in Washington DC.).

Once at Beckley, I was welcomed by a friend of mine I've met back home at the United States embassy when I was applying for my visas. He was there for the same reason and through him I found out about "Mountain State University" which I finally enrolled in. Thimothee Gansonre was his name, he was just granted his visas the day we met at the embassy and was supposed to travel the oncoming week. I was so impressed by his success that I tried to stay in contact with him even after he left. We chatted through e-mail and he promised to help me with my application for admission. Timothee stayed at a motel room where he worked for an Indian businessman in the city of Beckley. Timothee wasn't staying on campus like most students because he needed to work in order to pay for his tuition.

Just like me Timothee's parents were not wealthy enough to support his full tuition in America. We shared a one bed motel room with bath and no kitchen. I promised him that I would pay half of the rent as soon as I get a job and he agreed. Couple of weeks later things started to get though, I was being asked by timothee to pay my part share of rent. Without a job there was no way I could've get such money then I accelerated my job search;........ Walking miles, going from store to store asking for job and willing to do anything that could get me an income. Beckley is a beautiful but tiny town that I liked with no public transportation. There was couple of international student from Burkina Faso enrolled at MSU (Mountain States University) but it seemed like we lived in a completely different world because most of them stayed on campus helped financially by parents or relatives.

Mountain States University "MSU" was a private nonsectarian not-for-profit university based in Beckley, West Virginia, United States. According to certain news, the University has ceased to operate effective January 1, 2013 and all degrees conferred on or before December 31, 2012 are valid and were received from an accredited institution. MSU was previously listed as one of the best universities in the Southeast by the Princeton review. The school had also been named a Military friendly school by G.I. Job MSU.

While in Beckley I met many young men from Ghana, Mali, Gambia most of them came from wealthy families or were given opportunities for a good start in America. I still remember them like it was yesterday among them was Isaac from Ghana, Moussa Sidibe from Mali, Musa Sagnia and sisters from Gambia, Obed from Cameroon. I still remember some good times spent together at a birthday party on campus where I was about to get kicked out of the building for drinking a can of beer that I brought from outside. I was asked by the security guard to throw my can before I could access the building. We played soccer most of the time and most of them were good players

Most of these students were not worried about how to pay for rent or tuition. Most of them had cars while driving was still a luxury for me, something I could maybe get one day if my America dream came to success I thought. Intellectually, I was above all of them and none of them had the value of the high school diploma I brought in America because one of the best in that region of Africa. I thought of playing basketball at some point and could've play in the school's team but unfortunately, the school required that only students who started their major could join the team.

So me being a foreigner taking English as a second language was a disqualifying raison. I wondered what speaking English and playing sport has in common. I couldn't file a claim because in a bad position to claim anything in America at the moment due to my F1 status. That's when I started getting hit by the so-called discriminatory requirements of the American Society. Requirements mostly customized for the sole goal to exclude.

Political Asylum

On September 22, 2010 I was granted a political asylum status in New York city based on my past student activism in college back in Burkina Faso. Just like any other asylee, I've been granted asylum based on fear of prosecution by a dictatorial regime back home. A new window has opened with new opportunities in sight in the same time. I was now able to get a driver's license, a work permit and even a green card couple of years later. It was a very hard and a lengthy procedure which took me three years to get

69

a simple approval. First I believed in what I was doing and then I worked to make it happen.

After one semester spent in school, I left Beckley to pursue my real goal and live the life that I was meant for in the United States. I decided to face my destiny like a man in America. For such, I had to be honest with myself, take risks, accept my situation then face my new reality. Also, my relationship with my friend and roommate Timothe Gansore in Beckley deteriorated because I could not pay my share part of rent, I was simply asked to leave. I spent couple of days negotiating with him to just give me sometimes because I just got a job and worked for wendy's somewhere in east Beckley. I was unsuccessfully able to convince him then i packed my stuff and went back in Philadelphia with an idea in my mind to start my asylum case which I knew would be hard be not impossible. I gathered all information needed to succeed.....

I hired an attorney and an interpreter from Philadelphia to represent me on the case then I wrote my version of the situation that he was going to defend at the immigration office and later in front of a judge. While on that procedure I needed a job, save money to pay for those services. I did almost all type of job while in this procedure, from fast food worker like "Wendy's" to jobber at a bakery in Philadelphia and New York. When I entered my asylum case, I worked at a bakery located in Philadelphia's suburb called "LEBUS BAKERY". "Le Bus Bakery" looks like a Malian business because most of the employees are citizens of the west African country of Mali. I was laid off from that job for the simple raison of poor performance which I did not agree with but still had to obey because I did not have a full legal status exempt from restrictions. I

was still on a student status even though I wasn't illegal. I ended up back in New York at some point where I stayed with a cousin of mine Aguibou Traore who was granted a similar case couple years earlier in New York City. Couple of weeks after my arrival in New York, I was hired by Fat Albert Inc., a Lebanese business located in Brooklyn. I saved money while I worked there and sometimes traveled back and forth between New York and Philadelphia to meet with my attorney Mr James Pittman who had his office located in Downtown Philadelphia. I didn't want to change my attorney and wanted to work with the one that started the case because I believed he would better handle it knowing my specific situation already he would've better defend me. The course of events later will prove that I wasn't wrong at all keeping Mr. Pittman as my attorney because we greatly won the case against the Government attorney.

I had a very strong case and I knew it because of my past involvement in student strikes back in Africa either in high school or in college. Plus, the former President of Burkina Faso was the very contested dictator Blaise Compaore who Killed one of the most renowned revolutionary President in the history of Africa Thomas Sankara to become President of Burkina Faso. A short biography of the revolutionary President: Thomas Sankara was Born on December 21, 1949, in Upper Volta formerly Burkina Faso; died in October 15 1987 in Ouagadougou.

Captain Thomas Sankara was the leader of the Burkinabe Revolution. In the former Upper Volta known today as Burkina Faso, a group of men decided to launch a revolution that would enable the country "to accept the responsibility of its reality and its destiny with human dignity". Thomas Sankara belongs to the group of African leaders who wanted to give the continent in general and their countries in particular a new socio-political dimension.

Thomas Sankara was the hope of the African youth before being coldly murdered by his best friend Blaise Compaore. Born in Yako, Upper Volta now Burkina Faso on December 21, 1949 was a charismatic left-leaning leader in West Africa. He was sometimes nicknamed "Tom Sank". He was considered by some to be an "African Che Guevara" A captain in the Upper Volta Air Force, he was trained as a pilot. He was a very popular figure in the capital of Ouagadougou. The fact that was he was a decent guitarist and liked motorbikes may have contributed to his charisma. Sankara was appointed Secretary of State for Information in 1981 and became Prime minister in 1983. He was jailed the same year after a visit by Jean-Christophe Mitterrand. this caused a popular uprising. A coup d'Etat organized by Blaise Compaore made Sankara President on August 4, 1983, at the age of 33. The coup d'Etat was supported by Libya which was, at the time, on the verge of war with France in Chad.

Thomas Sankara saw himself as a revolutionary and was inspired by Cuba and Ghana's military leader, Flight Lt. Jerry Rawlings. Many wondered at the time if he wasn't just overthinking his ideas or day dreaming. The revolutionary President meanwhile has never been more serious in his projects and he always worked to make them happen As president, he promoted the "Democratic and Popular Revolution" RDP (Revolution Democratique et Populaire). His government included large number of women. His policy was oriented toward fighting corruption, reforestation, averting famine, and making education and health real priorities. Improving women's status was one of Sankara's explicit goals, that was unprecedented in West Africa. His government banned female circumcision, condemned polygamy, and promoted contraception. The Burkinabe government was also the first African government to claim that AIDS was a major threat for Africa. In 1984, on the first anniversary of his accession, he renamed the country Burkina Faso, meaning "The land of upright people" in Mossi and Dioula, the two major languages of the country. He also gave it a new flag and wrote a new national anthem. On October 15, 1987 Sankara was killed in a coup d'Etat organized by his former colleague Blaise Compaore. A week prior to his death Sankara addressed people and said that "while revolutionaries as individuals can be murdered, you cannot kill ideas".

He was so committed, he died for the cause he believed in as a real revolutionary person and only few African pan-Africanists can equal him. Not to wonder why President Blaise Compaore was so contested later in power by Burkina Faso youths.

President Thomas Sankara

Blaise Compaore then spent twenty-seven years in power before overthrown by an uprising by the people of Burkina Faso in October 2014. As a reminder, Blaise Compaore came to power by a "coup d'etat" through which he'd killed his best friend Thomas Sankara in 1987. Since then, he stayed in power for twenty-seven years, spent his time manipulating the constitution of Burkina Faso in order remain the President. Under his regime later there had been a lot of murders and killings of civilians mostly student activists. ... Dabo Boukary, a young student of the University of Ouagadougou died tortured by the Miliary as well as Flavien Nebie, a young man who was killed during a student strike. Then Blaise Compaore's brother Francois Compaore was also involved in the torture and killing of his driver whose name was David Ouedraogo. All sign prouved that the regime was dictatorial with ties with western countries like France, Belgium and the United States. I still remember an interview of mine given to an online press of Burkina Faso called burkina24 in 2015 during which I talked about that tie between American politicians and the dictatorial regime of Blaise Compaore. That collaboration made me a target in the United States by those individuals for years. Something that the American media refused to denounce for years because accomplice themselves. A truth that they will try to unsuccessfully hide and destroy the evidence.

As my struggle continued, I always remained focus on my goal which was to obtain a legal status in the United States for better opportunities. Couple of days before the interview in front of the judge, things started getting worst. That is when I was illegally locked out by the Guinean landlord; I stayed in that basement apartment in fear until the day of the judgement. I woke up in the morning, wore my black suit and red tie with a gray paint that I had spare inside my suitcase for big events and parties. Then I've catched the train all stressed out because I was couple of minutes late. I was supposed to meet with my attorney Mr. Pittman at the immigration because he was supposed to travel down from Philadelphia. I finally made it and the two (attorney and interpreter) were already installed waiting for me to come. It didn't take that long; I was just asked couple of questions and my answers where translated to the judge. On the other side, there was the attorney from the Government who worked against my case by asking tricky questions. I properly answered to all his questions with no mistake. I was then declared my status by the judge as a political asylee then welcomed to America. The judge has signed an approval notice which I was given a copy by my attorney. I was so happy but didn't know it was just the beginning of my struggle in this country for many years to come. I wasn't still even close to see that American dream everyone look for. It was a little more opportunity administratively and less fear in front of authorities than before. From now on, instead of worrying about my student status, I can call myself legal with no restriction on my stay in the United States of America. I could also travel back and forth with no visas requirement to reenter the United States. "No visas requirement" just means that I do not have to apply for visas at the US embassy on my way back to the United States.

To travel abroad as an asylee, I just needed a travel document from the United States Immigration and naturalization service (USCIS). The asylum travel document looks like a U.S passport, the only difference is the color and the information inside which clearly shows an immigration status and indicate that it is not a United States passport. While abroad, the asylee is given a restricted time frame to reenter the country by the USCIS otherwise he may lose his/her asylum status.

Homeless man in America

At first, I was shocked by the fact that I was confronted with homelessness in the greatest country in the world. Prior to that, I knew that anything could happen to me in life from poverty to death but never knew I would be called homeless one day in my life. Then I had to deal with that new reality which transformed my American dream into an American reality and nightmare. Then I became the homeless man in other word, the invisible person in the

87

American society four years long. The saddest and malicious fact is that you become invisible just for the people around but visible to police and prosecutors whenever they need you. Which police never hesitate to harass the homeless for being poor, not having a place to sleep and asking for help. Yes! I have been a living proof of such humiliating harassment in the streets of Denver and Philadelphia.

It all started in New York city when my landlord, a citizen of the West African country of Guinea hired someone to attack me in an apartment that I was renting in his house basement. I paid Mr. Kante Mamadou $475 in cash every month for a room inside his house basement in the Cambria Height area of the

Borough of Queens. Inside that basement apartment he was illegally renting under New York city law at the time, there was three rooms, a kitchen and a bathroom that I was sharing with two other men. One of the room was occupied by his uncle named "Doumbia". It looks amazing to me how some people can be so greedy and mean in life. The rents he was collecting out of the three rooms could've cover his entire mortgage and bills while he lived on the upper level with his wife and kids. I trusted him as an African brother by paying him cash and never asked for a single receipt or proof of payment until he decided to forcibly remove me against laws and regulations. I guess he thought I was one of those illegal immigrants hiding so he could've done whatever he wanted and get away with it. But yet, I was not fully a permanent resident but I was not illegal either because I was still on process on my asylum case.

Mr. Kante Mamadou was so surprised when I called police after he's thrown all my belonging in the street of Cambria height. All my stuff was packed inside big black garbage bags and thrown in the street by the two men while I was waiting for police to come for help. When police came, He told them that he's

never seen me and that I never lived there. Later in court, he said that I never paid him a penny. In my turn, I defended myself in front of police as well as in front of the judge then won the case. I was just awarded $2100 which I believed wasn't fair for the damage which occurred on my belonging. I wondered why he wasn't punished for this criminal behavior as well. It just seemed to me like the man has paid my freedom, proud and dignity and it just cost him $2100. I'll never agree with this sentence and still believe he deserves to spend some times in jail for what he has done.

In 2008 I moved in New York city to pursue my asylum case which was on removal proceeding in the immigration office, I shared a two-bedroom apartment in Brooklyn with my cousin Aguibou Traore. Couples of months after my arrival in the city my cousin was scheduled to travel back in Africa on vacation. As soon I got in New York, I started looking for job going from door to door and asking people if they were hiring. Through my job search, I found myself in manhattan where I've seen a lot of young people standing with red and yellow jackets selling tickets to tourists for commission in exchange. I did not hesitate to approach them and get information on how to apply. I was referred to their main office where I was told right away that there were available openings. I was scheduled for an interview after which I did one week of training along with other young people. The name of the company was "City Sight New York".

I started working for City Sight as a ticket agent which is similar to sales person. As ticket agents for City Sight we stand in the street of Manhattan looking for potential tourists wishing to visit New York. We had tickets available to visit popular places like Empire State building, Rockefeller Center, Status of liberty, Nine eleven memorial, Brooklyn and many different places in New York. I was a very good sales agent making enough money for a beginner in that field but it didn't last long until I was fired from that job. Then I found a part time job at UPS which didn't last either. In December 2008 as scheduled my cousin left New York for Burkina Faso on vacation then I was in charge to pay his part share of the monthly bills for three months to his room-mate. I was just able to make a one month payment out of three when he came back. He was upset but there was nothing I could've done. He was so mad that he's packed my stuff out of the room that we shared together then put them inside the kitchen. I realized that he no longer wanted me there and that was the last time we've seen each

other since 2008. That move predicted all that followed next. I could not find my own place and live in peace for six months straight but wasn't still officially homeless until 2013 in Philadelphia.

I found an apartment at University city in Philadelphia near my dream ivy league school the University of Pennsylvania. I relied on my student loan which supposedly covers all expense of students including rent, meals, transportation, books and miscellaneous, tuition and expected to find a job by then. I applied for thousands of jobs but unfortunately was never called back and my awarded student loan could not even cover half of my rent.

In January 2013, I was evicted for non-payment of rent. That is when I officially became homeless in America then moved into a shelter in downtown Philadelphia called "Our brother's place". Before that, I had to go through a lot of administrative procedures starting at "Station house" in north Philadelphia then I was placed at "Our brother's place" later, transferred to "Sunday breakfast". Shelters in Philadelphia all looks like with almost same rules. Three meals are served a day, light goes on around 6:00 Am and out at around 8:00Pm. What shocked me the most was the required shower time when dozens of people shower in the same bathroom all naked and all together.

As an African, I was shocked, never knew it could happen. I've seen stuff that normally as an African should never see or go through until I die. There is no way you will see someone your dad's age naked in the same shower unless that person is crazy living in the street. One other thing in shelters in Philadelphia is how people are treated. No respect at all and always asked to leave the building no matter how cold it is outside. They rather leave the buildings empty until meals times or bed time at night.

Then I moved in Denver, Colorado couple of months later expecting a better situation but I guess it was worse. I stayed in shelters located in Downtown Denver like "Jesus save" which was at some point so crowded that many slept outside in the street. The luckiest were taken every day to a different location in the North-West part of Denver and brought back to the center city in the morning for just couple of hours of sleep.

Loss Prevention Agent

I became a loss prevention agent for Rite Aid around the second half of the year 2010, exactly that moment when I lost it all in the United States of America. All I had left was an asylum approval from the United States Citizenship and Immigration Services "USCIS" which was supposed to open doors to new opportunities for me in this country. Now that I have an official legal status, I could have access to public benefits like food stamps, health care and public housing. But my ambitious character was not

99

allowing me to even think about applying for those benefits because I believed such benefit to be suitable for elderlies and disabled individuals. I thought of getting a better job and start a new life. On my asylum approval package was included a list of references to access those benefits. The one I was interested in was a job training and placement for a new career. I went to a New York department of human services where I applied for a security license through that department because I was assigned a case manager to work with. Things went very fast and I finished my training days later, entered my license application and was approved. Once I received my license in the mail, I went back to my case manager who had a list of jobs opening available. I was soon scheduled for an interview to become a loss prevention agent for Rite Aid Corporation.

I was hired at the time when reports from retail Knowledge - producers of the largest risk and loss prevention conference series in the world took place. The report identified that United States retailers were losing $60 Billion a year to shrinkage, up from $57 Billion recently in 2014. Additionally, the report (US retail fraud survey) identified employee theft as the single biggest cause of loss to retailers. These are statistics of the N.A.S.P (National Association for Shoplifting Prevention): There are approximately 27 million shoplifters (or 1 in 11 people) in our nation today. More than 10 million people have been caught shoplifting in the last five years. Shoplifting affects more than the offender. It overburdens the police and the courts, adds to a store's security expenses, costs consumers more for goods, costs communities lost dollars in sales taxes and hurts children and families.

Shoplifters steal from all types of stores including department stores, specialty shops, supermarkets, drug stores, discounters, music stores, convenience stores and thrift shops. There is no profile of a typical shoplifter. Men and women shoplift about equally as often. Approximately 25 percent of shoplifters are kids, 75 percent are adults. 55 percent of adult shoplifters say they started shoplifting in their teens. Many shoplifters buy and steal merchandise in the same visit. Shoplifters commonly steal from $2 to $200 per incident depending upon the type of store and item(s) chosen. Shoplifting is often not a premeditated crime. 73 percent of adult and 72 percent of juvenile shoplifters don't plan to steal in advance. 89 percent of kids say they know other kids who shoplift. 66 percent say they hang out with those kids. Shoplifters say they are caught an average of only once in every 90 to 48 times they steal. They are turned over to the police 50 percent of the time. Approximately 3 percent of shoplifters are "professionals" who steal solely for resale or profit as a business. These include drug addicts who steal to feed their habit, hardened professionals who steal as a life-style and international shoplifting gangs who steal for profit as a business. "Professional" shoplifters are responsible for 10 percent of the total dollar losses. The majority of shoplifters are "non-professionals" who steal, not out of criminal intent, financial need or greed but as a response to social and personal pressures in their life. The excitement generated from "getting away with it" produces a chemical reaction resulting in what shoplifters describe as an incredible "rush" or "high" feeling. Many shoplifters will tell you that this high is their "true reward," rather than the merchandise itself.

Drug addicts, who have become addicted to shoplifting, describe shoplifting as equally addicting as drugs. 57 percent of adults and 33 percent of juveniles say it is hard for them to stop shoplifting even after getting caught. Most non-professional shoplifters don't commit other types of crimes. They'll never steal an ashtray from your house and will return to you a $20 bill you may have dropped. Their criminal activity is restricted to shoplifting and therefore, any rehabilitation program should be "offense-specific" for this crime. Habitual shoplifters steal an average of 1.6 times per week.

Through the hiring process, I successfully past the interview and background check, took an in-class training after which I was assigned to my first store located in east Brooklyn where I was supposed to be trained in-store by another agent before I could be assigned to my own store. The main duty of a loss prevention agent is to deter, investigate and sometimes arrest potential shoplifters in the store. For such, the loss prevention agent has access to a court circuit television monitor for the purpose of keeping an eye on all ongoing activities inside the store. He also has a duty to walk through the aisles and around the store to have physical contact with the store's mechandise and customers. Customer service is also part of the job.

The agent then report all activities to the loss prevention manager who's different from the store's manager and has his office outside the store at the loss prevention department. It is indeed a very dangerous job because the agent is not allowed to carry guns or any type of weapon while thieves could be armed. In case he makes an apprehension he's supposed to call police for the person to be taken into custody and taken to jail. That is the part where he cooperates with law enforcement outside the company like police.

Weeks later, I was assigned to my store where I worked along with another agent. As I was new on the job, I mostly followed and watched how he operates in that specific store because each agent also has his own way to operate and what matters to the loss prevention manager is result which means apprehensions. I remember to have been many times called on not having made enough apprehension by my manager Ron Harrison. From my first store I was able to make couple of successful apprehensions cooperating with store's staff I was transferred to another store located this time on Rockaway Parkway where I worked with two other agents. That location was a high theft hotspot in a dangerous neighborhood and the store's manager was Sharlyne Marsh, a young lady in her late twenties with a Hispanic complexion assisted by Shamaika Blue an African American young lady and two other assistant managers.

I was mysteriously fired by Mr. Ron Harrison and couple of Rite Aid managers for being non-productive right when I apprehended one of the biggest thief in Rite Aid history. A tall African American Black male making more money than the district manager by shoplifting at Rite Aid. The man was not just a shoplifter, he was a businessman and the day of his arrest he had $460 worth of item inside his bag composed of razors, lotions, soaps that he was selling in the neighborhood to females that works at beauty saloons. I still cannot explain as of today the reason why I was fired.

As a loss prevention Agent it's not obvious to have good work relationship with staff because you're also required to report whatever they do inside the store if suspicious. The relationship between the agent and the store manager is not always a good one knowing he has no authority on the agent and knowing that he could be reported by him at any time. I remember to have had a very conflictual relationship with managers and staff because I was the eye of the store and could report whatever they do to my manager. I also had the ability to see and record everything that happen in the store on CD's through my court circuit television. The staff which is composed of store manager, supervisors, cashiers is

110

required to cooperate with the agent. It is therein

hard to get their collaboration because most of the

time accomplice themselves.

Ivy league dream

In 2010 in New York city, after my grant for political asylum status, I thought of going back to school to get a college degree. I knew I would need a college degree at least to get a better job or to start a political carrier in America or anywhere else in the world even know college degree doesn't obviously mean potential. Also, in case I was to go back to my country one day for whatever raison, at least I would have something to show to my parents as an

113

achievement and work for my country. Please don't blame me because I am smart I always say to people…….

Ambitious I am, the first thing that came in my mind was an ivy league and the closest ivy league to me at the time was the University of Pennsylvania located in Philadelphia where I lived and hanged around for years. As soon as I was fired from my loss prevention job in New York City, I moved in Philadelphia to start that project. Philadelphia because I wanted to attend the ivy league but also Philadelphia because my long times friend, the one that I almost considered like a brother since Burkina Faso lived there with his entire family.

My dear friend Stephane Sankara, is a young man I've met since Africa more than a decade ago along with Gildas Babadjiou in Ouagadougou, Burkina Faso. It was around 1998 when I used to play for one of the most renowned basketball team of Burkina Faso at the cadet level when the two approached me in school because they recognized me during a basketball game and liked the way play. Immediately, we sympathized became friends then started hanging out together. There was three of us: Stephane Sankara, Gildas Babadjiou who was a citizen of Benin and Ismael Galbani who now lives in Germany.

Stephane's dad emigrated in the United States in the late heighty's I've heard and Stephane stayed with his mom and brothers in Burkina Faso while attending school. I happened to sympathize with the entire family and sometimes spent more time in their house than in my own. At some point, I felt like a family member and was very praised and respected by his mom among all other young men that also hang in there. We've done it all together like brothers despite our differences we stayed connected and

dealt with our problems as we could. We tried to find solutions on whatever divided us then moved on. When time came for them to emigrate in the United States to join they dad who lived there for years, I was on their side supporting them because I knew they'll have a better life with mom and dad around them. I helped their mom in filling up all their paperwork that came from the United States embassy because they all came in English. None of her kids had my level of education at the time whatsoever. I've used my basic English skill from college to help her. My friend Stephane, the oldest of the family was not much helpful to his mom.

When time came for me to think about emigrating in the United States, they were obviously the first people that came in my mind. I did talk to their mom about my project maybe she could give me a hand in return. She did what she could before leaving Burkina Faso and I am grateful for whatever she's done. I have personally learnt to never count on people one hundred percent in life because you may be deceived one of those days. I kept on digging on my own side with the little knowledge and resource that I had available to me until I was in my turn approved for a student visas just couple of years after they left. My Visas was approved in August 2007 just more than a year after they emigrate.

Stephane was the last of the family to leave Burkina Faso. I obtained my Visas two years before him then Later in 2009, he also received his visas then came in the United States. He came unhappy to have been left alone and blamed me to have given up on

118

him when I came in the United States because he was unware of the struggle I was going through in America. We went through couple of arguments when he came because he felt betrayed which is understandable to me; I said to myself he'll maybe understand later. When I moved in Philadelphia to attend University of Pennsylvania, I thought of staying in their house for a while until I get my own place but it didn't work the way I thought they dad didn't want me to stay. I stayed with his brother Richard Sankara in his studio apartment located in University City until I moved to my own place.

I came to realize that this friendship with Stephane was over and will no longer work because I

119

think we were people with different personalities something America helped us discover. Stephane worked in a car wash for years and is today in a relationship with a black African American lady he lives with since couple of years, they have two kids together. For someone with so much opportunities I find Stephane to be negligent and not ambitious enough to make a difference in life. He is too deep into alcohol and maybe drugs. This time of my life, I needed a friendship which is going to motivate and help me succeed not a friendship that is going to keep me where I am at because I came from too far and still have a lot to do in my life. The last time I visited their family in January 2016, their dad clearly told me I wasn't welcome anymore in their house and I respected his decision, apologized if something wrong I've done then left. I swear to never go back again in their house and I pray God to give me the strength to reject whoever reject me in life and to know the difference between my friends and enemies. Where I am at in the United States, I can't blame anybody for whatever I go through because I came here by myself and decided to stay. I am the sole responsible of whatever I do in this country, reason why I refuse to take responsibility for anybody's life or mistakes.

Despite the shock of feeling betrayed by my best friend and family, I still hanged on to my ivy league dream. I've been still looking for opportunities since I've been attending community college of

121

Philadelphia. Studying at community college of Philadelphia was as well a plan for me to get in as a transfer student at the University of Pennsylvania. Fact is that, I needed to pass a higher English level which I knew I had the potential to do but was placed in a class way below my normal level. My placement test at Community College of Philadelphia was a sort of block because I could only take math classes but i was stuck for the rest for years because of English. One of my greatest souvenir at community college is when I ran for President of the student Government association in 2012 but lost the election...... at least I tried. I said to myself that could've been the start of a great leadership carrier in the Country because out of that experience I gained confidence and realized that

I had some very powerful leadership skills and abilities.

I hate writing about bad souvenirs as I try to erase them out of my mind but my worst souvenir is when I got kicked out of my Math class by an Indian teacher in the name of Atish Bagshi. I wondered how this so-called Doctor in Math has made it through to become a college level teacher. It was either I was very good in math or he did not deserve the position he occupied at Community College of Philadelphia. His mistakes on tests were negatively impacting my grade to the point that I decided confront him and let him know. As result, he kicked me out of the classroom pretending I was disturbing the class. I filled a complaint on the issue but had no support from the school administration. I also hopelessly contacted local medias like Fox news, Nbc10 news, Channel6 for them to denounce the issue in the news for the American people to be aware of the ongoing situation. I was able to get in touch with a morning news anchor in the name of Tracy Davidson, very well known in the Philadelphia community but at the end nothing was done until I left Philadelphia. I felt like things just got worse since I talked to that lady. I suspected her to be part of the same freemason organization based in Downtown Philadelphia where most of our African leaders subscribe in and from where they seem to run African countries.

Among those so renowned African leader Freemasons who belong to the Phidelphia Grand lodge:

- Djibril Yipènè Bassolé, a Burkinabé politician and diplomat who served in the government of Burkina Faso as Minister of Security from 2000 to 2007 and as Minister of foreign affairs from 2007 to 2008. Following a September 2015 failed coup by the Regiment of Presidential Security which was closely associated with Compaoré, Bassolé's assets were among those frozen by state prosecutors. Bassolé was arrested on 29 September for allegedly supporting the coup.

-Ahmed Bakayoko, Minister of interior of Ivory coast under President Alassane Dramane Ouattara himself freemason from the grand lodge of Philadelphia. Not to wonder why the Ivorian President easily granted asylum to Blaise Compaore later when he was overthrown from his twenty-seven years Presidency in Burkina Faso.

-Ali Bongo Odimba, a Gabonese politician who has been President of Gabon since October 2009. Bongo is the son of Omar Bongo, who was President of Gabon from 1967 until his death in 2009. Those are the officially known by the public. Meanwhile, many African leaders regularly participate and take orders from their American mentors directly from that grand lodge of Philadelphia. Their patrons, their Gods are the so controversial Philadelphia politicians like the former mayor of Philadelphia Michael Nutter, the current district attorney Seth Williams recently fined over $60,000 fine for suspicious income and unreported gifts.

According to New England Grand Lodge Freemasonry means different things to each of those who join. For some, it's about making new friends and acquaintances. For others it's about being able to help deserving causes – making a contribution to family and society. But for most, it is an enjoyable hobby.

Our values are based on integrity, kindness, honesty, fairness. Freemasonry is one of the world's oldest and largest non-religious, non-political, fraternal and charitable organizations. It teaches self-knowledge through participation in a progression of ceremonies. Members are expected to be of high moral standing and are encouraged to speak openly about Freemasonry. The following information is intended to explain Freemasonry as it is practiced under the United Grand Lodge of England, which administers Lodges of Freemasons in England and Wales and in many places overseas. Freemasonry is a society of men concerned with moral and spiritual values. Its members are taught its principles (moral lessons and self-knowledge) by a series of ritual dramas – a progression of allegorical two-part plays which are learnt by heart and performed within each Lodge – which follow ancient forms, and use stonemasons' customs and tools as allegorical guides. Freemasonry instils in its members a moral and ethical approach to life: its values are based on integrity, kindness, honesty and fairness. Members are urged to regard the interests of the family as paramount but, importantly, Freemasonry also teaches concern for people, care for the less fortunate and help for those in need. If this information was accurate why are so many freemason politicians suspected or convicted of crimes like rape, pedophilia, murder, money laundering and more.

Among the suspected Freemasons surrounding Tracy Davidson there is an African American male co-anchor of Tracy Davidson called Vai Sikahema plus another young lady who worked at NBC10 as a traffic anchor. The network have been part of a very filthy project against me for years. Clearly, they may have been manipulated and used by my long-time detractors in America to use their devilish power against me. I kept this information secret as of today until I get real proof and evidence of my allegation before I decided to make it available inside my book. Those that unjustly worked against me in this country even though I am not an American by birth have always lost including Jillian Mele. Just couple of years ago, she was a traffic anchor for one of the greatest television channel in the United States and today, she's just a simple sport anchor called "Breakfast on Broad". Back then, she was respectable and respected but now found herself in the middle of some type of football stars playing childish on national television every day. I wonder if she gets the same respect from the American public as she did at NBC10 where she was a traffic reporter when I came in Philadelphia..

I came to realize that Philadelphia might not be the right city for me to live in despite my ambition to enroll at the University of Pennsylvania. Plus, the daughter of the dictator former President of Burkina Faso Jamila Compaore have been studying at the

University of Pennsylvania for years. This is known by many people in the African community something that American leaders and the Obama administration will once again try to deny or cover because of their ties with the Compaore regime. If I personnaly have a message for this Philadelphia Mafia, I would just tell them to go blame the people of Burkina Faso who overthrown their very protected daughter's dad from power. It all happened in Africa while I was in America so why I am I being targeted in America. The people of Burkina Faso did what they thought was right for them and their Country and they assume it.

Uprising of the people of Burkina Faso against the Compaore regime. October 30, 31 2015

That's pretty much how America protects the criminals and their families and expose the honest, the uprights. The university of Pennsylvania, this so renowned ivy league school I dreamed to attend for years. According to Forbes: The University of Pennsylvania is a highly competitive (both pre- and post-admissions), private Ivy League research university founded in 1740 by Benjamin Franklin. It continues its close relationship to entrepreneurs to this day and is the alma matter of many innovative CEOs and billionaires including Elon Musk, Google CEO Sundar Pichai, Tory Burch and Donald Trump. Penn is divided into four undergraduate schools - the largest of which is the College of Arts and Sciences - and offers specialized dual degree programs. The

Wharton School, the world's first collegiate business school, and the School of Nursing are praised as among the nation's best. Its Medical School is also the oldest in the country and was founded before the Revolutionary War. Penn hosts over 450 student-run clubs and organization, and almost a third of students participate in Greek life. The Quakers compete in NCAA Division I athletics. Football fans throw toast onto Franklin Field – the oldest collegiate football stadium that is still in use – after the third-quarter of games. Holding a $10 billion-plus endowment, Penn has an All-Grant Aid Program that provides traditional, undergraduate students with a financial aid award that includes only grants and a work-study job. There are no loans included in students' financial aid awards.

After the military, I came back to attend Community College of Philadelphia for the spring semester 2016. Two semesters later, I realized that the same system was still there with almost the same attitude because I wasn't still given enough fund to study despite the Government willingness to lend me money through federal student aid and direct loans. I applied at Delaware County Community College and successfully took the placement test with a higher level in English and math. That placement test reflects more my level than the one from community college. Whatever was holding me back at Community College of Philadelphia will no longer exist. From now on, I can take whatever college level class that I want in my new school then accelerate my curriculum toward graduation. However, my dream for an ivy league is still not dead as of today. Either Harvard, Princeton, Yale or other ivy leagues in the United States, I keep my eyes open on potential opportunities. One thing is for sure, more than one person will regret what they've done to me in the coming years when I leave this country. But first, I expect to finish my citizenship

in the coming months before I go visit my family in Burkina Faso sometimes this year.

American Soldier

Since Beckley West Virginia in 2007, I thought of joining the United States Military then I went to a Military recruiting station located in Downtown Beckley not far from a Walmart store to get information on how to join the Military. Despite my legal status, I was told that a green card was required to join the United States Military. I've been to many recruiting stations and met with dozens of recruiters signed documents and even took practice tests called ASVAB (Armed Services Vocational Aptitude Battery).

Later, in Philadelphia and New York I was told different things. I felt like I was already working in the Military because they were getting information through me every time I was meeting with them. I've been many times picked up from my apartment by recruiters and taken to their office making me believe that I was eligible for a program called "MAVNI". The "MAVNI" program was created to hire people who speak foreign languages in the military for such, they were not required permanent residency at the time, I was told that "MAVNI" was open to even international students. Recruiters I worked with always came up with different things which disqualify me but always manage to make me believe there was still hope. The last thing I was told was that there was a list of languages needed to qualify for "MAVNI" and none of the four languages I spoke was part of the list. I was lost at some point, reason why I decided to just focus on my asylum case which would've at least open more than one door to me in America. I knew however that something wasn't right with me being asked for a green card despite a legal status in order to join the military.

In September 2010, three years later I was granted asylum in New York. It happened exactly when I was on my knees in this country. I almost lost everything ..... I recently broke up with the woman that I mysteriously met, had a good relationship with her, trusted her and at the end found out she was fake. That same year I was evicted from my apartment by the Guinean landlord who didn't hesitate to break my door while I was asleep the pack my stuff inside garbage bags with no court procedure. It is as well in that same year that I'd lost the highest pay job that I ever had in the United States. ......I worked for a bakery in Jamaica Queens in New York city called Hostess. I was really down on my knees; I'd lost everything; I'd lost the most important things in life: job, relationship, apartment in the same year and almost at the same time. It was a big tragedy, something that I'll have to deal with for the rest of my life because as of now in 2017 I still remember each of them like it was yesterday. The only thing that could've relieve my pain at the time was my asylum grant. It just seems like sacrificing my life and dignity just to stay in the United States because I felt like I was dead from who I am but lived for just one thing "America". I tried hard to convince myself that whatever happened was just my destiny or maybe "Karma" but I did not believe to have done so bad in my life to have had to pay so much. I also knew a lot of people who's done worse than I did in life but never went through such situation. At some point I started believing and having more and more evidence that whatever happened was motivated and purposely done. By whom?? I couldn't tell because I was so confused and left by myself. I was then left alone standing against an invisible enemy who could be anyone from my past relationships seeking revenge, my last employers fearing lawsuit for unlawful terminations or the Guinean landlord against whom I'd entered and won a civil lawsuit in New York City. But yet, I was still not allowed to lose hope at that crucial moment of my life, I needed to remain focused in order to make it because it was only me facing the United States of America with bunch of hostilities around a whole lot of enemies.

According to statistics from the United States Immigration services, millions of immigrants are admitted each year in the United States and thus for many reasons. Not to include Mexicans illegal immigrants that walks throughout the border. At the end, they become such a burden for the country that

I believe is the reason why the US Government gets involved in many conflicts around the world. That's pretty much one reason why I decided to pursue my application to join the military after I was granted asylum. I thought it was a good idea to get involved and help my new country in solving problems just like they helped and accepted me. I was then willing to forget and forgive whatever happened in my life and serve my new country that I call my adoptive country.

Once in Philadelphia, after I registered for school at Community College of Philadelphia in 2011, contacted the Army recruiting station in North Philadelphia not far from Community College of

Philadelphia then I was asked couple of questions like my immigration status, my level of education and my arrest record. Then I was asked by the army recruiter in the name of Sergeant Garret, an African American young man who was a snipper in the army to come over with my documents. As usual, I was there with all my paperwork in hand thinking that everything was ok and I was good to go. I catch the Market Frankford line from University City in South West Philly to downtown then I transferred to the broad street line northbound. The recruiting station was so easy to find right by Temple University. As soon as I walked in, I had that same sensation like before and every time I went to a recruiting station. The offices looked like same with the American flag and soldier posters all around. At the front desk there was a white male in the name of Sergeant Wallet then there was Sergeant Garret the person I talked to over the phone. I gave him all my documents... he looked at them then said everything was good but I needed to get my college transcript translated from French to English. As usual he'd made copies of all my documents then gave me the originals back. I'd sent my documents for translation weeks later then went back to that same location but surprisingly, Mr. Garrett denied to have ever met me before despite my effort to remind him on who I was. I had to resubmit all my document again to him and he'd made copies of them again. This time I was already seeing myself in that uniform and serving.... Too quick, I was now told that my asylum approval was not enough to join the military, this time and once again I need a green card before I could join. I was so disappointed after that because it takes at least two years from an approval in order to get a green card. I worried about getting older or becoming demotivated before I get my green card. I stayed in touch with my recruiters however knowing I was not being treated right asking me all that in order to join the United States Army, also I had information on people that joined without a green card when the United States needed soldiers in war time.

At some point, I realized that I was just being played by those recruiters because if the main goal of hiring a soldier was to kill why should one be required to have a clean background in order to join the military. Why would a simple jail record disqualify one from joining the military if he is to be hired and trained to kill?? And why is the person recruiting me who's a sergeant with at least five tour in Afghanistan who'd already killed at least ten people still there....No! no! and no! I said to myself, something wasn't making sense. But as a good investigator I didn't want to make any conclusion without real facts and evidences. Also, I wanted to go until the end of what I've started. I also wondered if the military was so praised in America why are there so many veterans homeless inside shelters, in the street with serious health issues from wars. .....why are they denied benefits by the department of veterans affairs knowing that they

151

should've been the first priorities of the nation they fought for. Personally, why was I so mistreated (arrested and charge by police for trespassing on my own campus) at some point despite my willingness to serve the greatest nation on earth. So many questions remained unanswered in my mind before my official enlistment in the United States Army.

On January 6th 2004, I was finally able to swear in and officially join the United States Army with an active duty status "11 X-RAY INFANTRY" Echo Company then was shipped down to Fort Benning for Basic Training. To me I was already serving them for years because a lot of documents were signed prior to that day. So I just considered that day as the day I officially joined the United States Army. I'd swore in Denver, Colorado but was shipped from Fort dix Pennsylvania where I started the procedure and took my physical test. We were dozens of soldiers at the Philadelphia International Airport traveling to Georgia for the new adventure to start. From the Atlanta International Airport, we've been picked up with couple of military buses then taken to the military base located miles away from the city of Atlanta. Once at the reception we were assigned units where we were supposed to stay couple of day until we get all paper work done and until were issued uniforms and all military gears necessary for training. On day one at the reception, we were already soldiers of the United

153

States army and that is when our active duty service starts.

A week later, we were brought into the barracks where we would spend the rest of the Basic training. We were split out into four different platoons and each platoon had around fifty to sixty soldiers. To each platoon, it was assigned three drill sergeants to closely follow the training. Drill sergeants are the closest leaders to soldiers and they report to the commander in chief. I still remember drill sergeant Erickson, a white male, in his forties very strict and drill sergeant Ortiz who was an African American very tall man in his late forties as well. They were both very good in terms of physical training but in terms of leadership I believe that they still have a lot to learn. Their bad leadership and mismanagement pretty much leaded to my discharge couple of months after enlistment. I was a very good soldier and it could've been felt already through my performance. I had one of the best PT (Practical Training) scores of my platoon. They were only few that could've match my score in the entire company and I'd proved it. At some point, I was assigned to duty of platoon leader and I did my very best in that position of leadership.

The drill sergeant decided to switch later then it was given to a black young man whom for whatever raison got into an altercation with me. It started a very heated argument which was about to come a Physical fight when other soldiers jumped between to separate. I'd filled a report on the situation and wanted to know what was happening because I felt some type of disdain from other leaders who preceded me. It felt like they were either jealous of the position of leadership I was given or they were just against it therefore were seeking revenge at some point. I tried to follow up on the situation that is when I was told by drill sergeant Erickson that all the soldiers were against me that all of them said bad

thing about me. I still remember that phrase of the drill sergeant just like it was yesterday.

Also, one thing that came in my mind is that sergeant Garret from the Philadelphia recruiting office challenged me during a random conversation then threatened to keep me from graduating once at Fort Benning. He immediately called one of the drill sergeant before I left then gave him some sort of instruction. I didn't pay attention to the details and was so confident that nothing could keep me graduating. I guess I should try to find out who the sergeant was communicating with. They seem to have a very powerful network in place which is in charge of sending soldiers then get them discharge later with the collaboration of some drill sergeants who work with them at the training station. It shouldn't happen that way because the soldier is sent to training to learn not to force him/her to quit. On the first half of March, right on the blue phase and after the hardest part of the training has passed, I decided to stop training because I thought unnecessary and even risky for me train alongside with people I can't trust anymore, people who for whatever reason started feeling disdain toward my person. And it all happened at that exact time when we were shooting the AK47's at the range. I just refuse to fight alongside the enemy because at the end, an enemy I would've been seen then targeted. That wasn't just why I joined the military and I wasn't willing to risk my life for a game if a game it was. By joining the United States Army, I took my decision very seriously, I was determined and focused while on training at fort benning because I really wanted to become the best. After many unsuccessful attempts to send me back to training either by drill sergeant or the commander in chief, I was officially separated on March 22 2016 along with dozens of soldiers most of them for medical raisons. I made sure that I left with my separation documents in hand because I didn't want to be mistaken with someone who went on "AWOL" (Absence without leave). In case of "AWOL", the soldier may be subject to persecution by authorities.

As of today, I have a status of veteran of the United States Army despite the country leaders effort to make all traces of my service disappear. I was picked up in the street in the center city Philadelphia while panhandling days before 2016 DNC (democratic national convention) and taken to a veterans transitional housing program down in North East Philadelphia. I am chocked recalling what is said in the soldier's creed, recites out loud by all recruits from the recruiting station until graduation because it is said to be the Army values. I went through some serious mental and psychological challenges, some real campaign of intimidation, harassment and even worse. I guess I went through what 22% of American soldiers go through and at the end commit suicide; the only difference in my case is that I thought about everything but killing myself because I knew that even after the military I still have a bright future ahead of me. I resisted and kept all records of my service including couple of pictures I've taken inside the barrack and I still have them posted on social media. Those are stuff that belong to me and shouldn't been taken away by anybody. I'll make sure that I keep these as souvenir until I leave this country or die. The only thing that I am proud of out of this adventure is my personal courage and accomplishment no matter my specific situation in this country, I resisted and fought. Because at end of the day:

I'VE BEEN THERE, I'VE DONE IT AND I AM PROUD.

162

Fort Benning Military base Georgia, US
Private Soldier E-2

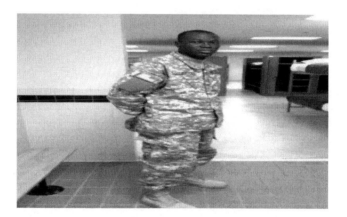

Contracts and agreements being signed between the two country's Military forces.

United States-Burkina Faso

166

Life in Denver, Colorado

In May, 2013 I moved in Denver, Colorado from Philadelphia. The main reason I moved in Colorado is because I found one the cheapest school in the United States through my searches on collegeboard then I decided to apply while I was still a student at Community College of Philadelphia. My application was approved the same week I applied. Then I decided to move to Denver with the purpose of earning more college credit before my enlistment because I was still

167

on a waitlist on my procedure with the Army. Couple more credits would've help me get a higher rank after my enlistment. Also, A little break from that city of Philadelphia where I first became homeless ever in my life couldn't been a bad idea.

Around the second half of May after my acceptance for admission at Colorado Heights University, I bought an Amtrack train ticket the same week then was on my way to Denver via Washington DC. It took us about 48hours with a stop at Omaha where I met with my friend from Burkina Faso Sosthene Compaore. Couple of minutes later we were back on our way through Mississipy where I've seen the Misissipy river for the first time. My fisrt impression of Denver was a beautiful city in a different style from the one in the east coast. I've catched the bus that goes directly on campus because I planned on living on campus which had some very affordable rent at about $350 a month. Thinks went so fast, I was welcomed and signed my lease the same day. I couldn't move in until the next day and it was snowing. That is when I discovered for the first time a motel called "Motel Six" where I was going to stay until the next day. Just like I lived in Denver for years, I had no problem getting around and coming back at Colorado heights University campus.

As soon as I moved in, I thought about transferring my Pennsylvania Driver's license. I went to the DMV with my immigration documents handy and had no trouble with the procedure. Couple days later, I received my Colorado Driver's license in the mail. At some point, I knew that I was followed by the same enemy because of whom I went through situations that leaded me into homelessness. I'd filled a report with the Federal Bureau of Investigation (FBI), hoping that something will change. I visited their office and met with a special agent with whom I went through the entire situation. Unfortunately, the FBI seems to be an agency that operates in the invisible on issues. Things started getting complicated when I spent all my savings and the school was putting pressure on me for my bills. Normally, I shouldn't have a problem because I had a consistent financial aid package. Unfortunately, a hold was purposely put on my financial aid by the internal revenue service (IRS) when time came to provide documents for verification. Despite all my proof of tax payment to the school they still wanted an original from the IRS. There's nothing I could've done because the IRS didn't want to release my record. I received a notice of eviction and had to vacate the school premise. I had nowhere to go and police was called on me while I was in the building by the school's security officer.

The first time I was ever arrested in my life and charged with trespassing on my own campus. I was taken to jail like a vulgar criminal a locked up for five days. One of the worst souvenir that I ever had in my life. I was ashamed to see myself among all these carrier criminals wearing those yellow jail clothes and presenting myself in front of a judge to explain to her that I was just arrested on my own campus because I was evicted from my apartment and had nowhere else to go. I was released the same day with a new court date to appear. I was confronted again with homelessness in my new city but fortunately, I found a job in downtown Denver at a 7-eleven store as a cashier.

The 7-eleven store was owned by an Ethiopian lady in the name of Aregash who didn't hesitate to hire me when I explained my situation to her. I saved money then prepared myself to leave for the Military. I worked for her three months long signed my contract with the Army then came back in Philadelphia to finish the procedure. While I was on procedure I'd met an African young man from Cameroun who was also interested in joining the military but didn't know how to proceed. I referred him to my recruiter and he also started the procedure. He was so happy that he suggested to share his two-bedroom apartment with me for a $400 monthly payment. I've made a first month payment with no issue while I worked at 7-eleven, on the second month, I was told to find another place because he needed the room for a lady who wanted to rent it. I was surprised and shocked because it happened right when I was organizing myself and I had only two month lefts from training. I asked him to put the lady on hold for just two months until I leave then he could rent the room to her, he refused. I got until an argument, he'd called police on me then I asked for a refund on my previous rent paid to him so that I could find myself a motel room for the rest of the week. He agreed and my stuff were packed in less than an hour for a new adventure. Nothing changes in my new city and I had to go back in a homeless shelter to stay until January 2014 when I leave for the military. I explained the situation to my manager Aregash, then traveled back to the east coast to finish the procedure with my primary recruiter.

After my discharge from the military, I came back in Denver but this time, I thought I was a free man and things will get better. Aregash had no problem hiring me back because she knew me as a dedicated and hard working person. I slept only one night out of three and most of the times I stay inside the train from the first train station until the last stop just to past time and stay warm. I had a gym membership with "Bally's" in Englewood where I work out a little bit and take a shower to stay clean. I had police following me like a high-profile criminal not even allowing me in public places. I thought about registering for school again and this time at Aurora campus in Downtown Denver.

My application was accepted in a bachelor program majoring in computer information system at Metropolitan States University of Denver. My transcript looked good when I transferred my credits from Community College of Philadelphia and University of Ouagadougou. That's when I found out my credentials were under evaluated at Community College of Philadelphia since 2011.

While on the right path to success, the invisible enemy kept his plan in action. For the second time, I was once again arrested by a campus police officer in the name of Jason Skeen while on campus. The officer openly violated my right, dumbed all my belonging on the floor despite my effort to explain my situation. I was handcuffed, physically brutalized because pushed down to sit on the floor and taken into custody. I was charged with trespassing, interference with a police officer etc.. On my appearance in court, I was asked to plaid guilty and accept to perform public service for the court to clear my record. I refused to put myself into a situation of "Self-incrimination" because, the punishment wasn't fitting the crime if crime there was for sure. Once I was released, I knew my life in Denver was threaten because that night when the officer approached me in the dark on campus could've been my last one. I knew that he was sent on my way and the goal was to do worse than just to arrest me. Mr. Jason Skeen's intention was clearly to eliminate me. I was just smart enough to have not resisted the arrest otherwise I could've been counted among all those black people shot by cops in America.

Not trusting the criminal justice system of the state of Colorado anymore, I decided to do some researches on my own then I found out Colorado was a high spot of the intelligence community for the United States Government. Some google searches shows that the CIA (Central Intelligence Agency) planned to relocate the headquarters of its domestic division which is responsible for operations and recruitment in Denver. The same information is confirmed in a Washington post article Published on Friday, May 6 2005.

According to the Washington Post article: "The CIA has plans to relocate the headquarters of its domestic division, which is responsible for operations and recruitment in the United States, from the CIA's Langley, Va., headquarters to Denver, a move designed to promote innovation, according to U.S. intelligence and law enforcement officials. About $20 million has been tentatively budgeted to relocate employees of the CIA's National Resources Division, officials said. A U.S. intelligence official said the planned move, confirmed by three other government officials, was being undertaken "for operational reasons." A CIA spokesman declined to comment. Other current and former intelligence officials said the Denver relocation reflects the desire of CIA Director

Porter Goss to develop new ways to operate undercover, including setting up more front corporations and working more closely with established international companies. Associates of Goss said Thursday that the move also was in keeping with his desire to stop the growth of CIA headquarters and headquarters- based group-think, something he criticized frequently when he was chairman of the House intelligence committee. Other CIA veterans said such a relocation would make no sense, given Denver's distance from major corporate centers. "Why would you go so far away?" one asked. "They will get disconnected." The main function of the domestic division, which has stations in many major U.S. cities, is to conduct voluntary debriefings of U.S.

citizens who travel overseas for work or to visit relatives, and to recruit foreign students, diplomats and businesspeople to become CIA assets when they return to their countries. It was unclear how many CIA employees would relocate to Denver under the plan. Spokespeople for U.S. Sens. Wayne Allard, R-Colo., and Ken Salazar, D-Colo., said they had not heard of the CIA's plans. State House Speaker Andrew Romanoff, D-Denver, said state leaders have worked hard to bring more jobs to Colorado, but "we just never thought to ask the CIA." "I've always thought that Colorado is the center of intelligence," Romanoff said. "I'm glad the feds finally realized the same."

Aurora Mayor Ed Tauer said he had heard that a branch of the CIA was moving to the region, but he had no information about where it would be located or which division would move here. "I think it's fabulous," Tauer said. "It would be great for the entire region. It would bring quality jobs and the contractors and businesses that come with them." Denver Mayor John Hickenlooper was out of town and couldn't be reached for comment. Gov. Bill Owens declined to comment on the report. Although collecting information on U.S. citizens under suspicion for terrorist links is primarily an FBI function, the CIA also may collect information on citizens under limited circumstances, according to a 1981 executive order. The exact guidelines for those operations are spelled out in a classified document signed by the CIA director and approved by the U.S. attorney general. It is unclear how a move to Denver would increase the effectiveness of the domestic division's operations, said several former intelligence officials. Colorado has become a major intelligence hub since the Sept. 11, 2001, terrorist attacks.

Aurora is home to the little- known Aerospace Data Facility. Located at Buckley Air Force Base, it has become the major U.S.-based technical downlink for intelligence satellites operated by the military, the National Security Agency and the National Reconnaissance Office, according to military and government documents obtained by William Arkin, author of "Code Names," a book about secret military plans and programs. About 70 miles south of Denver, the U.S. Northern Command, based at Peterson Air Force Base in Colorado Springs, is tasked with homeland defense and has been increasing its domestic intelligence work. It's not known if the CIA's Denver plans are linked to the presence of either facility. The Denver move, which is tentatively scheduled for next year but has not been finalized, coincides with several other developments related to the CIA's domestic intelligence work. Last week, the CIA and FBI agreed to a new "memorandum of understanding" on domestic and foreign operations, the first change in decades. The negotiations surrounding the memo were contentious, with the FBI saying that it should control and approve the CIA's domestic activities. But the FBI is having significant problems developing its own domestic intelligence branch, and the CIA is generally viewed across the intelligence community as more experienced and skilled at handling foreign informants."

It all proves that the CIA may have been relocated already in 2013 when I moved in Denver and may have targeted me as a foreign spy. Now I started worrying about my life in that city. I could've been right or wrong thinking so but time wasn't to think but to act as quickly as possible. I wrote a letter to the judge in charge of my case then the next day I was back in the east coast. However, my investigations won't stop right there for sure until I am sure of what really happened in Denver leading to my arrest and prosecutions. I became a private investigator working on a strong case with no real support.

Later, I found out the CIA just wanted to work with me once they discovered my potentials and values, they wanted me to join the Organization but didn't know how to approach me with their proposal. Instead of negotiating, they used strategies like bullying, intimidation etc... Once I realized they real motive, I stopped worrying then things started to come to normal. Not that I am denying they offer, but I thought it could've been done officially in a different manner with respect and consideration to my person. My integrity is inalienable to certain limits as I live with respect of certain values just like Thomas Jefferson said in one of his most popular quote: "In matters of style, swim with the current, in matters of principles stand like a rock".

In May 2015 I've filled a lawsuit against the United States Government through the United States Court of Appeals for the Federal Circuit. The case was closed without good cause because the Obama administration was avoiding confrontation well aware of the situation. The Obama Administration meaning the Democratic party has always been behind pushing to destroy. They needed a cover up of their bad leadership by pushing Hillary Clinton to become the President. The next document is the first page of the case that I've entered against the United States Government : Abdoul VS. United States.

Abdoul Ouatthema Vs. United States

NOTE: This disposition is nonprecedential.

United States Court of Appeals
for the Federal Circuit

ABDOUL K. OUATTARA HEMA,
Plaintiff-Appellant

v.

UNITED STATES,
Defendant-Appellee

2015-5053

Appeal from the United States Court of Federal Claims in No. 1:15-cv-00055-FMA. Senior Judge Francis M. Allegra.

Decided: June 8, 2015

ABDOUL K. OUATTARA HEMA, Philadephia, PA, pro se.

ANNA BONDURANT ELEY, Commercial Litigation Branch, Civil Division, United States Department of Justice, Washington, DC, for defendant-appellee. Also represented by BENJAMIN C. MIZER, ROBERT E. KIRSCHMAN, JR., MARTIN F. HOCKEY, JR.

Before NEWMAN, SCHALL, and HUGHES, *Circuit Judges.*

Ouatthema Intelligence

Ouatthema Intel is a private consulting agency that I've created when I left the military in April 2015. It is registered within the common wealth of Pennsylvania department of State under the status of sole proprietorship. I am also currently seeking a registration within the USPTO (United States Patent and Trademark Office) for my trademark to be official.

The agency's logo consist of a capital letter «I» cercled with a letter «O » , a standing squirrel In the middle, on the lower bar of the letter «I» ;   ..Colors are blue, black and red. The agency's emblem is a standing squirrel with crossed arms. I am inspired by squirrels as symbols of courage, knowledge, intelligence and freedom; those are qualities that I also rely on for better results as I take my job and duties more seriously than anything else.

The agency's motivational quote is Result matters to me and i always have them. The meaning of this quote is that no matter the outcome of the result that you get in life, whether positive or negative as long as you learn from it then it matters. In July 2016 I've clearly established the agency's terms and policies. Those are rules that will be followed throughout my cooperation with other structures in the coming years. I want my agency to become international and work beyond the American borders in the future.

Logo of Ouatthema Intel

Ten years spent in the United States working for various companies with almost no reward at the end, I decided to create my own structure and become self-employed. At first, I wanted to help law enforcement in the very continuity of my carrier as a veteran of the United States Army and a former loss prevention agent with a registered security license from New York States. Then I realized at some point the complexity of helping people that works against you and even unjustly target and prosecute you throughout the country. I will never forget the harassments of the American police in Philadelphia and Denver that I've been through. I decided to be realistic with myself, forget the past and put my skills in service of those who'd appreciate it.

As I write this amazing book right now, I am preparing a press conference in the month of November 2017. It's going to be about introducing Ouatthema Intel to the American public, the release of the book The Dirty Political Game "My Life" followed by a powerful motivational speech. I'll hold the conference at Delaware County Community College which is my new school. The name of the event is "LET'S FACE THE NATION". Let's face the nation because I decided to speak up from now on and refuse to be silent after so many years living like a prisoner in this country. I will face the American authorities and their law enforcement organizations no matter who they are if necessary and expose the truth if needed.

When thing goes wrong, time comes to situate problems and take responsibilities for a new start. It's just called justice. That is also a proven procedure even in the field of medicine the doctor has to make a diagnosis, know the disease before he can prescribe medications.

Surprisingly, I found out a similar event has been scheduled by a United States Navy Seal in the name of Shannon Rush on January 25, 2017. At 9:00 am, I jumped inside the Market Frankford line in direction of Delaware County Community College to assist the event. It took me a while to find the small auditorium at the college, then I found it couple of minutes later. By the time I to stepped aside to smoke a cigarette, order my student ID Card, it was already 11:00 am and the event already started. The speaker went through his personal life story when he was young, his military training and service and spoke to motivate the audience.

Despite all that Mr. Shanon Rush claimed to be, he surprisingly didn't have any story of struggle and personal accomplishment to share with the public. It just tells me that he still has a lot to learn in life in this country. Then came time to ask questions but we were told to be quick because the speaker was to assist another event later. After I introduced myself as a veteran of the United States Army and went through a little bit of my life story and struggle, I asked him what was his thought on veterans and service members being denied benefits by their own Government. His answer was that he did not join the Military for benefits but joined the military to serve his country. A legitimate answer I thought for someone who claim a status of a warrior but not honest enough to convince me. Then I asked him if he wasn't paid while he was in service and if he would've serve without a pay. My question stayed unanswered because obviously, no one would serve for free in America or nowhere else in the world.

I was then told that he was running out of time, that we could talk about it later at the veteran center. At the veteran center later, we just had time to take couple of pictures and that was it. I congratulated him because he had a relatively good audience inside the auditorium but still did not agree with his answers. How can someone pretend to be a navy seal in service of his nation and feel indifferent to whatever veterans go through being a veteran himself. With no intent to judge him on his decision, I expected a better answer from him than the one that he gave to his audience to be honest.

My event's advertisement has already started on Facebook and I created a special page for it. I worked on the posters myself on my laptop computer which I plan to post on many locations around the city. Now is time to start looking for sponsors for the event then I'll also contact the school to make a reservation of the auditorium where the event will take place. I plan to invite city officials, military officials if needed, law enforcement officials, American media, and all my sponsors to the event.

Veteran In The Streeet

After years of homelessness labeled as an invisible person in the American society despite my level of education and veteran status, I decided to leave the shelters and stay in the street. I slept inside parks daytime, under the bridge at night and panhandle to survive. I bought myself a sleeping bag then slept in despite the freezing temperature of the winter time. It was damn freezing while I stand with my sign in the street and at some point, thought I would've die if I didn't go through military training earlier. It's been very embarrassing for me at first but when time come in life when someone reach such point, there's no more shame or proud; you just have to do what it takes to survive. I made a lot of money sometimes, even more than what I was earning at my minimum wage job at 7-eleven. I was harassed by police and got into serious argument because of them trying to dissuade me with the fact that panhandling was against the law. Finally, the only reason I even able to sneak around was because other Americans were doing the same thing in that same area. I've made videos of them, recorded their voices and threatened to file a lawsuit for harassment and discrimination against cops that approached me. I've been shown my place in the American society since the last four years, something that I will never ever forget in my life and I intent to stay where I am at until I get my citizenship in the coming months. If I didn't die from what I've been through in last four years, I wonder if I'll ever die again.

I realized that everything was done for me to repeat the same mistake that got me arrested in Denver. I resisted and stayed away from criminal activities no matter the pressure. Obviously, when people look at me, they realize that I deserve better, that I am not like other homeless in the community. And I also know that it is just a matter of time and I'll be out of this mess. At some point I was confronted by other homeless doing the same thing. Either because they did not believe that I was a veteran or they just didn't want me there because I seemed to receive more help than they do. I even got into physical fights despite my effort to peacefully deal with them. It was just the street and no one's property and everyone has the right to stand in the street I always try to explain because no one owned the street.

Finally, I found a place in front of a retail store called "Target" where I stay every day because I get along with the security team of that store. They understand that I am not there with bad intention. Police at some point followed and tried to remove me from there as well but the security team oppose to that and even store associates take my side. I am thankful to those young men working in that location. It is herein important to point out that some cops were also nice to me and treated me fairly. I remember a lady from the Philadelphia Police Department who bought me food once and never ask me to leave. I also have good connection with some outside security people that monitors the parking lot. Because of Maria, a beautiful Spanish and nice lady, I was never bothered by those as well.

As of today, January 2017, I am grateful for things getting better in my life. I am enrolled in a veterans transitional housing program located in Northeast Philadelphia where I share a room with a sergeant of the United States Army. We share a kitchen and a bathroom with two other veterans in a Unit. I was on a lower floor couple of months ago then moved to the second floor. I've been promised to get help with housing later. But once again my eligibility would be very limited because of my length of service. I was told by my case manager that they could provide me with a security deposit and maybe a first month payment. That wouldn't be a bad idea at all if I get an income before I move. As I've learnt in life to never count on someone hundred percent not even the Government I also look out for state and federal benefits like healthcare, food stamp etc... I applied and receive $195 each month for food stamp and I also have healthcare which helps me a lot with my breathing issue; It covers part of my expenses on an inhaler.

It hasn't been easy coping with other veterans at impact mostly because I am the only African and others may have problems understanding my service in the United States military. I do my best in trying to fit and make them understand the situation. That's all I can do because I cannot be responsible for anybody's ignorance in his/her own country. Since I've been at impact, I went through three major altercation with other veterans. The first one was an elderly veteran I was roommate with who was very provocative. The second was a special forces veteran younger white guy who tried to rule my life by telling me exactly what to do even on my personal time. I couldn't done anything inside the room without him complaining..

The next day, I asked to be given a different room. The third incident was an African American man who sniffed drugs then went crazy all night. He would get naked then try to force people to have sex with him. Apparently, none of us was amused by the scene then he was removed by police and discharge the next day. I wondered what he had against me personally shouting "The African guy". However, I understand that many people in the program may have health or mental issues.

I've been walking approximately ten miles a day since the last strike of Philadelphia public transportation workers (SEPTA). I stay connected with whatever I've been doing to survive and refrain to live like other veterans in the program who get an income from the Government because they retired in the military. Most of the veterans living at impact are

elderlies which means that they had time to live their life until retirement, now they seem to have nothing to lose by spending all day long watching TV and eventually socializing in the community.

In my age, with everything going on in my life in this moment, I can't afford to live like a retired person.

209

I still have a lot do before I reach the age of retirement. I also need to stay focus on what happened In my life, what I have been doing to survive in case I am to go back in the street for whatever raison. I should be able to stop panhandling as soon as I get an income and an apartment. Then my life will considerably change and I will be able to live a normal life like anybody else in this country. Most importantly, I've learnt something that if you're not careful in America you could lose everything by the clap of the hands. A great nation of immigrant is also where you'll see all type of people from different belief and background. I've learnt to protect my belonging, fight for what I believe is right and fight against what I believe may be wrong. As long as what

210

I do remain harmless to others I'll never hesitate and I am definitely not ashamed of anything I do or have done at the moment in my life. Very cautious right now, no real friend or partner in my life, I am the happiest person on earth despite all that I went through. My life is just beautiful as it is right now and I'll never let no enemy destroy it again.

The picture ID on the next page has been issued to at the Delaware County Government center. It's an identification card issued to recently discharged Military service members. To receive this ID, the requirement was to present a DD-214 without a dishonorable discharge and I do have a DD-214 with an uncharacterized discharge which means neither honorable or dishonorable. I noticed a mistake on my first name so instead of Abdoul it clearly shows "Addoul". I decided then to go back and have it fixed. That is when it was taken back pretexting that my discharge had to be honorable. I had the requirement sheet handy showing clearly "Other than dishonorable". The ID being just a privilege not a right, there's nothing that I could've done. Meanwhile I decided to keep a picture of it as a souvenir because the picture at least belongs to me and it cannot be taken back. It's still me against them I guess.

Veteran Identification Card from the Delaware County Government Center

Dolce Vita in America

Despite all the stress that I went through in the United States, I always managed to find myself sometimes to enjoy life. That was the only way to show the enemy that I wasn't desperate, to show the enemy that I was so strong that none of his attempts to destroy me would work. In other words, I kept my head up and fought for what I believed in the United States of America.

In 2009 I traveled down to the state of Georgia to meet with my beloved girlfriend Paula Black Tatum. Paula was the love of my life I thought, a beautiful white Caucasian with blonde hair. She looked younger than I despite the fact that she was ten years older than me and was a single mom of two. Age don't matter much when two persons love each other and that is a fact. She had a very good job in Atlanta when I worked in a retail store in New York as a sale associate. She was the one to pay for my plane tickets and all expenses when we meet. I never had to spend a penny because she wouldn't even let me to. She owned a house in the suburb of Atlanta where we went to once but most of the time, we rented a hotel in Atlanta to stay in.

We had some very good times together with Paula in Georgia. The only problem with Paula is that she was being manipulated by the invisible enemy. At some point, she wanted a child "in vitro", that's something that I didn't want to do because I really did not believe in such practice to be appropriate. However, Paula was more than a girlfriend for me she was a good friend of mine beyond intimacy.

When I left the military, I bought my first car a two door "Buick" sport fashion. It was a used car but I loved it because it was my first that I'd purchased out of my own pocket. The simple feeling of having done something by myself, for myself, for my own pleasure was enough for me to feel happy and proud.

I spent time in one of the most expensive hotel in the United States located in Downtown Washington DC non-far from the white house. From my hotel room, I watched the white house a mile away from the window while I admire the beauty of the city.

I also party a lot when I came back in Pennsylvania, I moved in Media located in the suburb of Philadelphia, one of the most beautiful place that I've ever seen since I came in America. I call Media my hometown because I will be moving in there sooner or later. Not just that it is beautiful but it is also quiet and peaceful. I used to party every week-end at a club called Jocklyn's and other bars around. I'd met some very nice people who at the end became friend with. We spent new year eve 2015 together with my friend Mike Mc Connell, Jenny, Carlos and other guys at Mike's house. It was unbelievable that night, none of us knew another before but we had fun like people who knew each other for years and stayed friends since then. I found out later that Jenny was from a very racist white Caucasian family and it hurts me when she told me her parents told her to not date black people. I was shocked when she told me that but never blamed her because she may be different from her parents and she proved that on new year eve by her friendship, good mood toward all of us. Among us was Carlos, a blind man in his forties who, despite his handicap was well praised by women. I always found

219

him surrounded by females anytime I meet him at the bar. He does everything like normal people do and travels a lot throughout the country to teach as an instructor.

When it comes to Philadelphia, I had also fun at one of my favorite night club called "Blue Martini with people from a completely different background and lifestyle. Blue Martini, the same club where I was clearly asked to leave the bar years ago by a Nigerian security guard who thought that I stink (smell bad). Now that I bought myself a $75 worth of perfume from Sephora, I am no longer bothered by security guards at "Blue Martini". All my suits and pants are bought from "Macy's" and my jeans from "American

Eagles". I am not rich but anytime I have a chance, I make a difference in the way I dress and speak unless I decide not to for a specific reason. I am not desperate as they want me to seem.

In April 2016, I bought a plane ticket to Tampa, Florida to visit my brother in law and my step sister who came in the United States in 2013 with both of their children Josey and Alisey. I couldn't wait to see one of my family member since nine years. The night before seemed as long as a week in my eyes. I stayed in a motel in Media called "Raven Motel" owned by an Indian businessman which cost $59 per night. At around six in the morning, I catch the 101 trolley to 69th street then transferred to a taxi cab which cost me more money compared to the SEPTA bus that goes straight to Philadelphia International Airport. At 8:00 Am I was at the airport ready to board and once inside the plane, I called my brother in law to confirm my arrival this time because at many attempts I'd scheduled and canceled my trip. This time, I told him I am coming to Florida and I'll be there in couple of hours. They were so happy to know this time I was coming to Florida. My first impression of Tampa from the Airport still flashes back in my head when I think about it.

Tampa, Florida felt like a completely different country, the climate was so tropical with trees everywhere around. I was spoiled five days long eating African foods, finally living a family life since I came in America. It was my first time meeting my nephews because they were born abroad before they

came in the United States. My step sister has changed, she gained a lot of weigh probably because of motherhood. Her and my brother in law became too religious in my point of view so their lives were bounded by a lot of restrictions and rules based on their religious belief. For example, we had to pray on the food every time we go on the table that's something that I haven't done for years. I lived the American way of life with fast foods and no time to waste. They live a very decent life inside a two-bedroom apartment with their two kids. A simple and

223

impressive lifestyle for people who just made it to the United States.

My trip to Florida has been full of enjoyment until I left. It was a great vacation time and I enjoyed it. I promised my step sister to come back anytime I'll get a chance. She wanted me to move to Florida but I have so much stuff to do in the east coast that I declined the offer otherwise it wasn't a bad idea at all. Five days later, I was back in Philadelphia because school was also still in session at Community College of Philadelphia.

Best friend Paula with kids in Atlanta, Georgia

American politics and immigration

In November 2008, a year after my arrival in the United States, America elected its first black President, Barack Obama. He was the winner after an election in the polls against the former secretary of state Hillary Clinton. The event was celebrated everywhere around the world, in Africa, Europe, Australia, Asia, America .... Newborn babies were given the name Barack because people seen in the first African American President a messy, a savior, some even compared him to Martin Luther King Jr.

227

Height years later, that enthusiasm evaporated into acynical disillusion. Barack Obama was not who the American people and the entire world thought he was or would be for the world in the next height years on the top of the greatest nation on earth.

A biography of the first black President in the American history relating to many sources: Barack Hussein Obama II was born on August 4, 1961, in Hawaii. His parents, who met as students at the University of Hawaii, were Ann Dunham, a white American from Kansas, and Barack Obama, Sr., a black Kenyan studying in the United States. Obama's father left the family when Obama was two and, after further studies at Harvard University, returned to Kenya, where he died in an automobile accident nineteen years later. After his parents divorced, Obama's mother married another foreign student at the University of Hawaii, Lolo Soetoro of Indonesia. From age six through ten, Obama lived with his mother and stepfather in Indonesia, where he attended Catholic and Muslim schools. "I was raised as an Indonesian child and a Hawaiian child and as a black child and as a white child," Obama later recalled. "And so what I benefited from is a multiplicity of cultures that all fed me."Concerned for his education, Obama's mother sent him back to Hawaii to live with her parents, Stanley and Madelyn Dunham, and to attend Hawaii's prestigious Punahou School from fifth grade through graduation from high school. While Obama was in school, she divorced Soetoro, returned to Hawaii to study cultural anthropology at the university, and then went back to Indonesia to do field research.

Living with his grandparents, Obama was good but not an outstanding student at Punahou, played varsity basketball and, as he later admitted, "dabbled in drugs and alcohol," including marijuana and president of the prestigious Harvard Law Review for the academic year 1990-1991.

Although Obama was a liberal, he won the election by persuading the journal's outnumbered conservative staffers that he would treat their views fairly, which he is widely acknowledged to have done. As the first African American president in the long history of the law review, Obama drew widespread media attention and a contract from Random House to write a book about race relations. The book, *Dreams from My Father: A Story of Race and Inheritance* (1995), turned out to be mostly a personal memoir, focusing in particular on his struggle to come to terms with his identity as a black man raised by whites in the absence of his African father. During a summer internship at Chicago's Sidley and Austin law firm after his first year at Harvard, Obama met

231

Michelle Robinson, a South Side native and Princeton University and Harvard Law School graduate who supervised his work at the firm. He wooed her ardently and, after a four-year courtship, they married in 1992. The Obamas settled in Chicago's racially integrated, middle-class Hyde Park neighborhood, where their first daughter, Malia Ann, was born in 1998 and their second daughter, Natasha (called Sasha), was born in 2001.

After directing Illinois Project Vote, a voter registration drive aimed at increasing black turnout in the 1992 election, Obama accepted positions as an attorney with the civil rights law firm of Miner, Barnhill and Galland and as a lecturer at the University of Chicago Law School. He launched his first campaign for political office in 1996 after his district's state senator, Alice Palmer, decided to run for Congress. With Palmer's support, Obama announced his candidacy to replace her in the Illinois legislature. When Palmer's congressional campaign faltered, she decided to run for reelection instead. But Obama refused to withdraw from the race, successfully challenged the validity of Palmer's voter petitions, and was easily elected after her name was kept off the ballot. Obama's time in the legislature initially was frustrating. Republicans controlled the state senate, and many of his black Democratic colleagues resented the hardball tactics he had employed against Palmer.

But he adapted, developing cordial personal relations with legislators of both parties and cultivating Senate

Democratic leader Emil Jones, Jr., another African American senator from Chicago, as a mentor. Obama was able to get campaign finance reform and crime legislation enacted even when his party was in the minority, and after 2002, when the Democrats won control of the Senate, he became a leading legislator on a wide range of issues, passing nearly 300 bills aimed at helping children, old people, labor unions, and the poor. Obama's one serious misstep during his early political career (he later called it "an ill-considered race" in which he got "spanked" by the

234

voters) was a 2000 Democratic primary challenge to U.S. Representative Bobby Rush. Rush is a former Illinois Black Panther leader who subsequently entered mainstream politics as a Chicago alderman and was elected to Congress from the South Side's first congressional district in 1992. Obama was not nearly as well known as the popular Rush, and the combination of his unusual upbringing and his association with predominantly white elite universities such as Columbia, Harvard, and Chicago aroused doubts about his authenticity as a black man among the district's overwhelmingly African American voters. Obama suffered what he labeled "a drubbing," losing to Rush by a thirty percent point margin. Returning to the state senate, Obama began eyeing a

2004 race for the U.S. Senate seat held by Peter Fitzgerald, an unpopular first-term Republican who decided not to run for reelection. In October 2002, as Congress was considering a resolution authorizing President George W. Bush to launch a war to depose the Iraqi dictator Saddam Hussein, Obama spoke at an antiwar rally in Chicago. "I don't oppose all wars," he declared. "What I am opposed to is a dumb war. What I am opposed to is a rash war." By speaking out against Bush's war policies, Obama set himself apart from the other leading candidates for the Democratic Senate nomination, as well as from most Senate Democrats with presidential ambitions, including Hillary Rodham Clinton of New York, John Kerry of Massachusetts, and John Edwards of North Carolina. Obama's initially unpopular antiwar stance eventually worked to his political advantage as the war became increasingly unpopular with the passage of time. Advised by political consultant David Axelrod, who had a strong record of helping black candidates win in majority-white constituencies, Obama assembled a coalition of

African Americans and white liberals to win the Democratic Senate primary with 53 percent of the vote, more than all five of his opponents combined. He then moved toward the political center to wage his general election campaign against Republican nominee Jack Ryan, an attractive candidate who, after making hundreds of millions of dollars as an investor, had left the business world to teach in an inner-city

Chicago school. But Ryan was forced to drop out of the race when scandalous details about his divorce were made public, and Obama coasted to an easy victory against Ryan's replacement on the ballot, black conservative Republican Alan Keyes. Obama won by the largest margin in the history of Senate elections in Illinois, 70 percent to 27 percent. In addition to his election, the other highlight of 2004 for Obama was his wildly successful keynote address at the Democratic National Convention. "There's not a liberal America and a conservative America," he declared. "There's a United States of America. There's not a black America and white America and Latino America and Asian America. There's a United States of America." Obama encapsulated his speech's themes of optimism and unity with the phrase, "the audacity of hope," which he borrowed from Reverend Jeremiah Wright. Wright was the pastor of Chicago's Trinity United Church of Christ, a large and influential black congregation where Obama was baptized when he became a Christian in 1988. Obama also used the phrase as the title of his second book, The Audacity of Hope: Thoughts on Reclaiming the American *Dream*(2006), which became a national bestseller in the wake of his newfound national popularity. Describing his religious conversion, Obama wrote, "I felt God's spirit beckoning me. I submitted myself to His will, and dedicated myself to discovering His truth."

I personally don't blame Barack Obama knowing politics and politicians myself. Also, him being the first African American President, it was obvious that he'd be challenged in many ways in the United States. It's clear that his leadership in office has been contested, manipulated by white extremists around him because they were not ready to accept a black President in office. I still remember politicians like Mitt Romney who created some devilish programs like "Self-deportation" under his presidency.

Here's the definition of self-deportation from Wikipedia that makes me cry and never want to deal with politicians: "Self-deportation is an approach to dealing with illegal migrants in the United States that involves the creation of legal structures which will make life in the US so difficult as to encourage illegal migrants_to voluntarily return to their home countries, rather than organized efforts of law enforcement to locate and deport them. It became associated with illegal immigration in the United States in the 1990s." I guess Mitt Romney ignore the existence of a structure called USCIS (United States Citizenship and Immigration Services) which is supposed to be the only organization to determine who's legal or illegal in America. I guess he also forgot that America was a country of law and democracy. Believe me, Mitt Romney is too smart to tell the

American people that the self-deportation program was instead meant for targeted individuals despites their legal status in this country. The republican party also knew what harm it would make to Obama's reputation if such program was to be applied so they played their political game. One thing is that Donald Trump should expect the same behavior from black extremist movements like "Black lives matters" and black leaders. The black life matter movement I believe is just a terrorist organization funded mostly by rich white people in other to mislead the youth by making them believe that everything that happen to them is because they're black. I am aware of the existence of racism still in America but I also believe that black people could make a difference by changing their mindset and do the right thing.

At the end of his two terms, I think Obama was one the worst President in the history of the United States not to wonder why his plan to impose Hillary Clinton to the American people during the 2016 election has failed. It was clear that democrats were just lying to the American people by playing two major cards; the one of gender by pushing women to testify against Donald Trump and by making immigrants believe that Donald Trump would deport them if elected. They wanted to make it look like Hilary Clinton was their best bet. History showed that

243

Democrats deport more than republicans and millions of immigrants were deported under Barack Obama. During the third and final presidential debate on 19 October 2016, Republican nominee Donald Trump remarked that President Barack Obama "has moved millions of people out … millions of people have been moved out of this country." As of 2015, more than 2.5 million undocumented people had been deported by immigration authorities since President Obama took office in 2009, a total which is indeed record-setting. During the two terms of his predecessor, President George W. Bush, just over 2 million people were deported. Newly released official figures show that during the first seven years of President Barack Obama's presidency, more than 2.7

million foreign nationals were deported — the largest number in more than a century. Figures contained in the 2015 Yearbook of Immigration Statistics, issued in mid-December, show that from the time Obama was inaugurated as America's first black president on Jan. 20, 2009, through Sept. 30, 2015, a total of 2,749,854 undocumented immigrants were removed from the United States. That's definitely a record in the American history.

The American people have seen through their plan and their intention to manipulate Hillary Clinton so that they could get some cover on whatever wrong they did while in office. Hillary Clinton could've also help Michelle Obama at her turn properly prepare to run for office in the coming years. Anyone with a basic knowledge on the American political era could see through her moves. I personally applauded the outcome of the election not just that I like Donald Trump or dislike Hillary Clinton but time was up for change and America could no longer afford to continue with a system which failed them for years. It is now up to the new President Donald Trump to proof that he was the right choice during his presidency. So far, many jobs and businesses that fled the country under Barack Obama are coming back and Donald Trump was the candidate that raised funds for veterans during the campaign. Not just that it showed that he was a great leader but it showed his willingness to work hard and help those who served this nation even before he became President. On the immigration issues as well, Donald reacted just like any leader with common sense who love his country would react. Immigration laws are clear and available to every immigrant either on their website or at the immigration offices. So every immigrant has the choice to either follow procedures, comply with the law and become legal or take the risk to hide from it then face deportation. How should one blame Donald Trump for trying respect his country's laws as the Commander-in-chief.

One of the biggest mistake of Barack Obama during his term is the step that he has taken to legalize gay marriage in the United States; him having sworn on the bible the very day of his introduction to the white house in January 2008. Anyone who read the bible knows that nowhere same sex marriage is allowed. Personally, I have nothing against homosexuals but I do not believe it should be a law in one nation under God. Everyone is free and accountable for his/her own sexuality in the United States so why was that needed. That was just another political set up he has failed to recognize and avoid.... Believe it or not it cost him a lot in terms of credibility.

Also, Obama spent too much time focusing his leadership on destroying and taking down African leaders instead of working seriously for the well-being of the American people. I remember he was involved with NATO (North Atlantic Treaty Organization) in the conflict in Ivory coast in 2009 when President Alassane Dramane Ouattara wanted Laurent Bagbo who allegedly lost the election to step down. He has also played a role in the killing of Ghaddafi which has been proven to be a wrong decision at the end. Why is America always supporting foreign countries in killing innocent people while inside their own countries while pretending to intervene for peace through its Military.

I understand the burden of leadership and no matter who you are as a leader, you cannot be appreciated by everyone because you'll never be able to satisfy everyone at the same time. However, I praised Obama when he suggested police reform when black people were being shot by police around the country. The American police definitely went out of control to the point that something needed to be done after the "baton-rouge" shooting in Louisiana.

One thing that no one will ever deny to Barack Obama is the fact that being the first black President has been the greatest accomplishment in history because ten years back, no one knew a black person would ever become President of the United States

especially one from African descent.

Barack Obama

Donald Trump

I could not finish my memoir without a short biography of the very impressive President Donald Trump who won the Electoral College with 304 votes against 227 for Hillary Clinton then became the President of the United States of America during the 2016 Presidential election. The triumph for Mr. Trump, 70, a real estate developer-turned-reality television star with no government experience, was a powerful rejection of the establishment forces that had assembled against him, from the world of business to government, and the consensus they had forged on everything from trade to immigration.

The unexpected American President who for sure still has a lot to do facing a very divisive Democratic Party still not aware of the message of the American people toward them. I think the message is as clear as the election has been. America is just tired of this Mafioso leadership from the top of the greatest nation on earth. A President should work for the entire nation not a group of people like African leaders.

According to many sources, the 45th President of the United States, Donald John Trump was born in 1946 in Queens, New York City, the fourth of five children of Frederick C. and Mary MacLeod Trump. Frederick Trump was a builder and real estate developer who specialized in constructing and operating middle income apartments in the Queens, Staten Island, and Brooklyn sections of New York. Donald Trump was an energetic and bright child, and his parents sent him to the New York Military Academy at age thirteen, hoping the discipline of the school would channel his energy in a positive manner. Trump did well at the academy, both socially and academically, rising to be a star athlete and student leader by the time he graduated in 1964. During the summers, Trump worked for his father's company at the construction sites. He entered Fordham University and then transferred to the Wharton School of Finance at the University of Pennsylvania, from which he graduated in 1968 with a degree in economics. Trump seems to have been strongly influenced by his father in his decision to make a career in real estate development, but the younger man's personal goals were much grander than those of his father. After graduating college, Trump joined the family business, the Trump Organization. In 1971 Trump moved his residence to Manhattan, where he became familiar with many influential people. Convinced of the economic opportunity in the city, Trump became involved in large building projects in Manhattan that would offer opportunities for earning high profits, utilizing attractive architectural design, and winning public recognition.

We still remember when the Pennsylvania central railroad entered Bankruptcy Trump was able to obtain an option (a contract that gives a person the authority to sell something for a specific price during a limited time frame) on the railroad's yards on the west side of Manhattan. When plans for apartments were refused because of a poor economic climate, Trump promoted the property as the location of a city convention center, and the city government selected it over two other sites in 1978. Trump's offer to drop a fee if the center were named after his family, however, was turned down, along with his bid to build the complex. In 1974 Trump obtained an option on one of the Penn Central's hotels, the Commodore, which was unprofitable but in an excellent location near Grand Central Station. The next year he signed a partnership agreement with the Hyatt Hotel Corporation, which did not have a large downtown hotel. Trump then worked out a complicated deal with the city to revamp the hotel. Renamed the Grand Hyatt, the hotel was popular and an economic success, making Trump the city's best known and most controversial developer.

Meanwhile Trump was investigating the profitable casino gambling business, which was approved in New Jersey in 1977. In 1980 he was able to acquire a piece of property in Atlantic City, New Jersey. He brought in his younger brother Robert to head up the complex project of acquiring the land, winning a gambling license, and obtaining permits and financing. Holiday Inns Corporation, the parent company of Harrah's casino hotels, offered a partnership, and the $250 million complex opened in 1982 as Harrah's at Trump Plaza. Trump bought out Holiday Inns in 1986 and renamed the facility Trump Plaza Hotel and Casino. Trump also purchased a Hilton Hotels casino-hotel in Atlantic City when the corporation failed to obtain a gambling license and renamed the $320 million complex Trump's Castle. Later, while it was under construction, he was able to acquire the largest hotel-casino in the world, the Taj Mahal at Atlantic City, which opened in 1990. Back in New York City, Trump had purchased an apartment building and the Barbizon-Plaza Hotel in New York City, which faced Central Park, with plans to build a large condominium tower on the site. The tenants of the apartment building, however, who were protected by the city's rent control and rent stabilization programs, fought Trump's plans and won. Trump then renovated the Barbizon, renaming it Trump Parc. In 1985 Trump purchased seventy-six acres on the west side of Manhattan for $88 million to build a complex to be called Television City, which was to consist of a dozen skyscrapers, a mall, and a riverfront park. The huge development was to stress television production and feature the world's tallest building, but community opposition and a long city approval process delayed construction of the project. In 1988 he acquired the Plaza Hotel for $407 million and spent $50 million renovating it under his wife Ivana's direction. It was in 1990, however, that the real estate market declined, reducing the value of and income from Trump's empire; his own net worth plummeted from an estimated $1.7 billion to $500 million. The Trump Organization required massive loans to keep it from collapsing, a situation that raised questions as to whether the corporation could survive bankruptcy. Some observers saw Trump's decline as symbolic of many of the business, economic, and social excesses from the 1980s. Yet Trump climbed back and was reported to be worth close to $2 billion in 1997.

Donald Trump's image was tarnished by the publicity surrounding his controversial separation and the later divorce from his wife, Ivana. But Trump married again, this time to Marla Maples, a fledgling actress. The couple had a daughter two months before their marriage in 1993. He filed for a highly publicize divorce from Maples in 1997, which became final in June 1999. On October 7, 1999, Trump announced the formation of an exploratory committee to inform his decision of whether he should seek the Reform Party's nomination for the presidential race of 2000, but backed out because of problems within the party. A state appeals court ruled on August 3, 2000, that Trump had the right to finish an 856-foot-tall condominium on New York City's east side. The Coalition for Responsible Development had sued the city, charging it with violation of zoning laws by letting the building reach heights that towered over everything in the neighborhood. The city has since moved to revise its rules to prevent more of such projects. The failure of Trump's opponents to obtain an injunction (a court order to stop) allowed him to continue construction.

President Donald Trump and Hillary Clinton

Social Network

I haven't been on social networks until I came in the United States in 2007. I personally started with HI5 while attending Mountain State University in Beckley, West Virginia then later Myspace in 2008 then Facebook and twitter more recently in 2009. I was then so surprised to learn that Facebook existed since 2004 and most of my friends were already using it in my first year in college since Africa. All I knew in Africa about the internet was to barely open, read and send an e-mail. The internet cost so much in this part of the world that these were the most that I could've done anyways being a student with no income or scholarship.

Now that I have resources available to me and a more advanced knowledge of the Internet, I wonder how much I was missing back in days. I think of all the things that were happening around me in my community and probably debated or published on the internet without me knowing. Before, my life was most focused on direct reality based on what I see and live on. The only source of information for me was the Radio, Television and newspaper but now I instantly have access to information all around the world through social network from the deepest corner of my apartment room.

To the question whether such discovery or use of the internet has benefited me in life the answer would be yes and no. Yes! because I am today in America because I once did some internet searches in order to find the school that I enrolled in the United States. And yes because without the internet I would not be able to access as many benefits and information available to me today. As we live in a high-tech world it is very hard to access information in real time without the internet. Not to wonder why most employers require an application for employment to be submitted online through their company's websites.

However, social network and the internet in General has had a very negative impact on my life in terms of privacy, fairness and accuracy of information. The example of Facebook where everything seems to be seen and known because of the Government and law enforcement agencies are also present. Social network became a working tool used for something other than socializing, a Spyware or maybe worse a mind control tool accessible to anyone, anywhere.

Facebook became life and life Facebook to the point that it seems to impact and determine political policies and decisions around the world. Many claim that Facebook has created revolutions in many Countries and has also impacted either negatively or positively Presidential elections. That being the case, I wonder if Social networks do not put our societies and forms of Government in jeopardy.

Mark Zuckerberg beside being a Billionaire became such a God for the entire world because everyone from the deepest South African village to the deepest city of Australia through the deepest State of America, everyone is connected and sharing information either accurate or not. People are drawn into some type of illusional relationships, fames and self-esteem. He is the God of anyone on Facebook

273

because he created it and has 100 percent power on one's information and privacy.

From now on the President may not be the most powerful person of the Country and his/her decisions may be undermined by random groups on social media. Social media for sure undermine the sovereignty of our forms of Governments hence created. That being said the creator of Facebook Mark Zuckerberg may have more power than the President of the United States and the world may end up having just one Government with Mark Zuckerberg on the top. If such is the case, borders, countrys, States may no longer exist. It is scary while many still use social network for fun because unaware of the impact on their lives, because unware of the changes that it could create around them, in their communities.

The other side of the impact of social network on our societies is also psychological as many people become addicted to the point that they entire lives seem to be resumed to that activity. Meaning that the brain gets so focus that it gets stuck to it. If social network is then not properly regulated those people would be reduced to only what they are shown and unable to think or make legitimate decisions on their own. My view of social network today goes beyond socializing there is something more dangerous happening behind those computer screens that needs

275

to be regulated for the good of the entire humanity in

the coming years.

Faith and Religion

I came from a big and very religious family with Islam as the most followed. My father is Muslim so was my deceased mother. That is one reason why I've been named Abdoul Karim since birth. I read the Coran and practiced Islam since my young age following my parents and didn't get to choose my own way until I grew up. I also went to church many times to pray and read the bible not just because I was a Christian but because I believe in one God for all religions and see the church and mosque as places to worship the same God. However, I was lucky enough to have had an open-minded father, mother and step mother and was never forced to worship their religion. As I grew up, I've learnt, became more responsible, free thinker then my entire vision of faith and religion has changed. I always believed in a higher power no matter the religion and I believe that higher power to be the so-called God that all religion believes in.

I just don't believe in religions and their practices. I believe in what's right and wrong and as human beings that belief is universal when it is not extreme or exaggerated. All religion on earth get to the conclusion that killing another human is a sin. And all of them praise their adepts in helping and supporting the needed and less fortunate. I wonder why there is so many conflicts based on religious beliefs while they all believe in one god. The only thing that should've divide religions is moral because moral depends on many things like background, race, ethnicity, education ..etc Not just because something may be seen as immoral by someone obviously means that it is bad.

Religions for me dehumanize the human and creates division among them not to wonder why so many wars going on around the world in the name of the same God. I see and praise religions as ways to connect, socialize when it brings messages of peace to the people. If religious people were perfect why are they so many pedophiles found inside the clergy in the Vatican. God himself seems not exempt from imperfection because looking at the world around you, you'll see a lot of thinks that shouldn't happen, a lot of injustices, inequalities but yet that's just life and nothing else.

As I am still in search of my real and own belief, I still have a lot of unanswered questions in my life. I had paid for whatever wrong things that I've done since I came in the United States. Sometimes even worst, I'd paid for the right things that I've done. It felt like I was being punished for being to good to the world and to the people around me. I have been punished for stuff that my dad or my family member may have done in the past whether right or wrong. I could've seen it myself as time pass. I could've seen alike faces from the past. I did not get away with a single lie or rudeness that I've said; it was all coming back to me at some point. Was that God punishing me? I wondered.

It has been said inside the holly books, we all pay after death whether we go to paradise or hell and God is supposed to be the judge. As far as I know, I am still alive but I was judged by human beings instead of God. I lived at some point without a single privacy, everything I've done was seen just like the "All eyes on me" sang by so many American artists. Maybe I live in a different and perfect world from now on where everything is known and seen but who's watching and for what purpose remains the question. Spiritually, I lived in a jail pretty much but I am soon to free myself. However, I'll be the last person to worry about people watching having no bad intention in my life. I live in peace with people around me if my life is valued and not threaten. In that new world if that is to be the case, I wish the eyes to be the ones of protection, justice, fairness not the ones of oppression or injustice.

Life back on track

My life is finally getting back on track and my American dream restored to where it was. It'll sure take time but most importantly it's happening. I've earned my first college certificate taking an online course from a school located in Ireland. I couldn've been more proud of myself to be finally able to show something professional beside my security license from New York State which expired couple of years ago. I applied for dozens of jobs and went to couple of interviews. The last on date was a supervisor position at Valley Forge Casino. I woke up in the morning and didn't know how to dress to look professional at the interview and didn't want to look too sharp for the position I was going to be interviewed for then I decided to be natural like I've always been and I guess it did work the way I expected it be. I was at Valley Forge, King of Prussia. I was at the casino two hours before my scheduled appointment rather than being late. I was just asked couple of questions during the interview to which questions I successfully answered. It's really promising and I am on wait for the rest of the hiring process in the coming days. I have also been scheduled for many other interviews with mostly security companies and hopefully I'll get hired by one of those.

I could not be totally restored without also a spiritual restoration I thought. So I went to church in this month, corresponding to lent in Christianity to ask the holy father for forgiveness, peace, wisdom in my life. I also prayed for the sick, the poor, the unfortunates around the world. May the almighty shows me the way in my pursuit of the American dream like he always did since the last ten years I said to myself.

As of today, I stopped walking as much as I used to because things are getting better. I haven't panhandled for a week, my time is spared between going to classes, writing my book, going to church and

285

looking for work. Those are undeniably signs of a better life in sight. I feel much better, mentally and spiritually more equilibrated than I used to be focusing on these daily routines. Things are also moving forward administratively as I received my long time lost documents from the United States Citizenship and immigration Services recorded on a 350 pages burnt on a CD Rom which contains copies of my Burkina Faso passport, I-94, birth certificate,

Asylum approval, military documents. I visited Burkina Faso embassy in Washington DC to be registered as a citizen and request a renewal of my passport. Meanwhile, I work on my name change procedure to comply with laws and procedures in the

United States of America. I came to realize that the most important thing in life is to get things done, things that can get you moving forward, things that can give you the feeling achievement. I believe in myself now more than ever but most importantly, I still let the higher power in control of my life. I see my days getting better and better, feel myself stronger, smarter and more determined to reach my goals from which I get close and closer each day and every day. The enemy, the devil has lost that game I've learnt to win ten year long through my struggle in the United States of America.

It's been a journey of struggle but nevertheless it's been a success story.

287

Abdoul S Ouatthema

****

This book intents to enlighten, inspire, inform and share a real-life Story with the world. A story of struggle and success of an African young man in the United States of America.

God help me during this journey. . . . . .

Abdoul S Ouatthema

AUTHOR: ABDOUL S OUATTHEMA

EMAIL: OUATTHEMAINTEL@GMAIL.COM
HTTPS://WWW.OUATTHEMAINTEL.COM

PHOTO CREDIT: FOTOLIA, GOOGLE
SOURCES; MEDIA, FBI, POLICE

70545572R00177

Made in the USA
Columbia, SC
09 May 2017